JOB
A MESSY FAITH

BY RON KECK
with Ben Colter and Derek Leman

JOB: A Messy Faith
© 2008 Ron Keck
Reprinted April 2012

Published by Serendipity House Publishers
Nashville, Tennessee

ISBN: 978-1-5749-4346-7
Item No.: 005038471

Subject Headings: BIBLE. O.T. JOB--STUDY

To purchase additional copies of this resource or other studies:
ORDER ONLINE at www.SerendipityHouse.com;
WRITE Serendipity House, One LifeWay Plaza, Nashville, TN 37234-0175

1-800-458-2772
www.SerendipityHouse.com

Printed in the United States of America

JOB
A MESSY FAITH

CONTENTS

Other great Serendipity Larger Story resources ...

MORE.

More depth, more meaning, more life.

Something inside us yearns for more from life, God, and Bible study than we've experienced Discovering truth through Bible study is more than breaking a verse down to its smallest parts and deconstructing a passage word-by-word. There is context and experience, mystery and story that all go into fully understanding the living Word of God. The essence of the whole is more than the sum of its parts. Serendipity acknowledges that story is the language of the heart, and, without it, we can miss the wonder and power of the message. MORE looks at the Bible and life within the context of the Larger Story—the eternity that God has written on our hearts. Dare to discover and experience more of life, more of God, and more of your role in the Grand Adventure!

Song of Songs: The Epic Romance 1574943405
Job: A Messy Faith 1574943464
Ruth: Gleaning Hope 141586702X

Mark: Beyond the Red Letters 1574943413
Colossians: Embrace the Mystery 1574944150

GOD AND THE ARTS

Where faith intersects life.

Stories, great and small, share the same essential structure because every story we tell borrows its power from a Larger Story. What we sense stirring within is a heart that is made for a place in the Larger Story. It is no accident that great movies include a hero, a villain, a betrayal, a battle to fight, a romance, and a beauty to rescue. It is The Epic Story and it is truer than anything we know. Adventure awaits. Listen.

Discover an experience that guides you on a journey into the one great Epic in which the Bible is set. These fun and provocative studies explore four films, each with two small-group meetings, *Dinner and a Movie* (Week 1), *Connecting the Dots* (Week 2), and an *Experience Guide* that offers valuable insights.

Finding Jesus in the Movies 1574943553
Finding Redemption in the Movies 1574943421
Finding the Larger Story in Music 1574944207

MORE.

In those rare moments of clarity we recognize that we want—no, need—more. Something inside us yearns for more from life, God, and Bible study than we've experienced. We sense we're more than we've become. We hope there's a lot more to God than we understand. And we need to believe there's more to the story than we've heard so far.

God dares us to desire more than a life of duty and obligation. Jesus didn't come to bring us more rules and regulations. He came to bring life (John 10:10) and invite us into a much larger story. Jesus referred to Isaiah 61:1-2 to describe His redemptive mission.

[17] The scroll of the prophet Isaiah was handed to [Jesus]. Unrolling it, he found the place where it is written: [18] "The Spirit of the Lord is on me, because he has anointed me to preach good news to the poor. He has sent me to proclaim freedom for the prisoners and recovery of sight for the blind, to release the oppressed, to proclaim the year of the Lord's favor."

LUKE 4:17-18, NIV

The MORE Series

The Larger Story into which we all were born is the greater, unseen reality that God reveals through Scripture and His Holy Spirit. This story includes perfect harmony and closeness dispelled by a failed insurrection ... the deadly fight between destroyer and redeemer ... paradise lost ... a beauty to be rescued ... the daring rescue under the cover of night ... ongoing dangerous battles ... final banishment of evil ... and the ultimate restoration of paradise. **Bible stories and teaching are set within the context of this larger backstory.**

Discovering God's truth from the Bible involves more than breaking verses down to their smallest parts and deconstructing a passage word-by-word. **The essence of the whole is more than the sum of its parts.** Traditional approaches to Bible study provide insight but can miss the magnificence of the forest while focusing on the trees. If we're not careful, we can drain the adventure and passion from Bible study and following Jesus, leaving us with details of duty and obligation.

God ... planted eternity in the human heart, but even so, people cannot see the whole scope of God's work from beginning to end.

ECCLESIASTES 3:11. NLT

Ecclesiastes explains why our hearts are moved by certain songs, dramatic movies, or stories. God has written eternity on our hearts so we resonate with its message. Jesus knew this and often used story to communicate because story is the language of the heart.

DANGEROUS ADVENTURES
AN EPIC
ROMANCE
VILLAINS & MONSTERS
TO BE SLAIN
A BEAUTY TO BE
RESCUED
BETRAYAL & INTRIGUE
BATTLES TO BE FOUGHT
AND WON
UNEXPECTED
TWISTS & TURNS
GOOD ULTIMATELY TRIUMPHS OVER EVIL
A HERO-REDEEMER
PARADISE
RESTORED

The MORE Approach

Traditional Bible study methods break passages into their smallest parts to gain insight and truth. There's some recognition of context (historical, literary, theological), but observation, interpretation, and application are seldom integrated with the Larger Story.

The key to the **MORE approach** is to start your study considering the elements of the Larger Story. Observation, interpretation, and application all emerge from the context of the Larger Story and lead toward heart transformation and life change here and now (Act III).

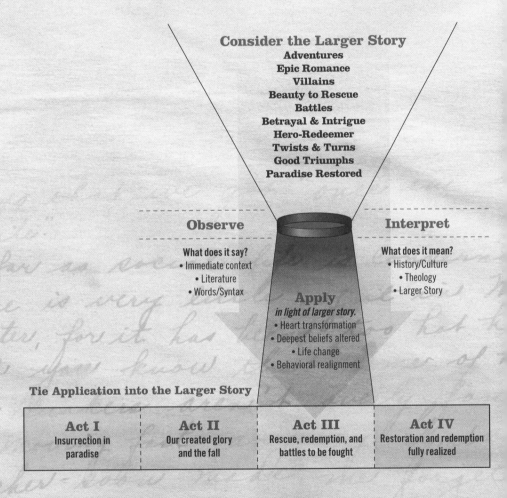

Consider the Larger Story
Adventures
Epic Romance
Villains
Beauty to Rescue
Battles
Betrayal & Intrigue
Hero-Redeemer
Twists & Turns
Good Triumphs
Paradise Restored

Observe

What does it say?
• Immediate context
• Literature
• Words/Syntax

Interpret

What does it mean?
• History/Culture
• Theology
• Larger Story

Apply
in light of larger story.
• Heart transformation
• Deepest beliefs altered
• Life change
• Behavioral realignment

Tie Application into the Larger Story

Act I	Act II	Act III	Act IV
Insurrection in paradise	Our created glory and the fall	Rescue, redemption, and battles to be fought	Restoration and redemption fully realized

This approach will train you to look at the Bible and life from the perspective of the Larger Story—the eternity written on our hearts. **MORE acknowledges that story is the language of the heart and, without it, we can miss the wonder and power of the message.** Dare to discover and experience more of God, more of life, and more of your crucial role in the Grand Adventure and Epic Romance.

JOB
A MESSY FAITH

Job's life became a train wreck; he struggled deeply with God. Unaware of events in the unseen realm, he was embroiled in a story far bigger than he realized. Job's story demonstrates that the life of faith is messy—raw. Our relationship with God is not fragile. Job poured out his hurt, anger, doubts, and disappointments to God ... and God loved Him for it!

The most basic interpretation we hear of the Book of Job is that it addresses the age old problem of suffering. All agree that Job helps us better understand why a good God allows suffering. Yet, for those who will take the unfamiliar paths out of their comfort zones, and for those who have eyes to see, the Book of Job has so much more to offer. As we reach beyond just another formula for theodicy, what **we discover is a raw, messy, redemptive journey into which God is inviting us**.

In this group Bible study on Job, you'll learn to wrestle with God. As you open the pages of this story together, you'll also discover that life is not about rigidly reigning in sin or upholding some moral code or "blessing formula;" it's about our relationship with the living God who adores us.

Larger Story Themes in Job

Session 1: PARADISE IN TURMOIL
  Insurrection; the Fall; Unseen Reality; Rescue; Eden Restored

Session 2: THE EPIC STRUGGLE
  Drama in Heaven; Shock Waves on Earth; Role in the Larger Story

Session 3: DARK SEASONS AND THE VILLAIN
  Villain—Fury & Fate; Strategic Attacks; Subtle Manipulation; Tactics

Session 4: TRUE LOVE AND DISTORTED LOVE
  Epic Romance; Pure Love; Distorted Love; Deception; Intrigue

Session 5: FAITH—REAL AND RAW
  Emotions Godly; Grieving Losses, Raw Feelings of Abandonment and Betrayal; Relationships vs. Formulas

Session 6: REDEMPTION REVEALED
  God is Wild, Unpredictable, Can't be Controlled; Passionate, Not Perfect

Session 7: LIGHT SHINES OUT OF DARKNESS
  Living Redeemer; Relent to God but Never Give Up; Redeemer's Heart

GROUP MEETING FLOW

OPENING SCENE

"Opening Scene" questions and experiences are designed to be fun and build community in your group. This helps put your group at ease and gets you talking casually about the day's topic. Everyone should participate so you can get to know one another and so you all can benefit from the diversity of stories and perspectives.

WHAT'S YOUR STORY?

Sharing your own story and listening to the stories of others will help you understand how your life fits into the Larger Story. Take time to discuss any key insights from take-home assignments, but focus on "Experience" or "Reflection" as noted in each session.

BEHIND THE SCENES

"Behind the Scenes" sets the stage for continued discussions about the Larger Story as they unfold throughout the session.

[LEADER: Invite volunteers to read various Scriptures throughout.]

UNFOLDING THE LARGER STORY

This section opens your eyes to the Larger Story of the epic struggle. Learn to see the truth of Scripture within the context of the Larger Story and then dare to question how your own story meshes with God's. As you embrace truth, you'll take steps toward a more passionate and personal relationship with God.

[LEADER: As a group, discuss as many questions as time permits. Be sure to highlight in advance the questions you don't want to miss. Try to keep things moving, but put the needs of group members ahead of completing an agenda.]

HEARTBEAT OF THE STORY

"Heartbeat" will help you connect with each other, with God, and especially with your own heart. A healthy small group should be a safe place for being open and real.

CONNECTING WITH MY STORY ...

Unique take-home assignments will lead you to go deeper with God and greatly enhance the overall experience of MORE.

DANGEROUS ADVENTURES

AN EPIC ROMANCE

VILLAINS & MONSTERS TO BE SLAIN

A BEAUTY TO BE RESCUED

BETRAYAL & INTRIGUE

BATTLES TO BE FOUGHT AND WON

UNEXPECTED TWISTS & TURNS

GOOD ULTIMATELY TRIUMPHS OVER EVIL

A HERO-REDEEMER

PARADISE RESTORED

PARADISE IN TURMOIL

A MESSY FAITH

Where were you when I established the earth? Tell Me, if you have understanding. ... Who stretched a measuring line across it? On what were its footings set, or who laid its cornerstone — while the morning stars sang together and all the sons of God shouted for joy?

JOB 38:4-7, HCSB

One day the members of the heavenly court came to present themselves before the LORD, and the Accuser, Satan, came with them. "Where have you come from?" the LORD asked Satan. Satan answered the LORD, "I have been patrolling the earth, watching everything that's going on."

JOB 1:6-7, NLT

LARGER STORY SYNOPSIS

We search for formulas to fix the messes all around us—in our world, neighborhoods, families, and hearts. The problem is that the Larger Story into which we've been born is in turmoil.

As we open the pages of Job's life, we find order, prosperity, peace, balance, and happiness—the life we long to live. God created us for joy and adventure, intimacy and ecstasy—for paradise, for Eden. Something inside us cries out for what's good and noble. We want the "blessing formula" to work! But just as in Job's story, life has been temporarily derailed. In the Book of Job, God graciously pulls back the curtain to reveal the unseen and shows how deeply it impacts our stories.

OPENING SCENE

5-10 MINUTES

TIME TO DIALOG

- GET COMFORTABLE WITH ONE ANOTHER
- EVERYONE SHOULD PARTICIPATE
- BEGIN TO SHARE STORIES AND EXPERIENCES

Burger King has an enticing slogan: "Have it your way." While this line might sell food, it just doesn't describe the way life typically works.

1. Take turns as you introduce yourself and tell the group about the biggest mess you recall making as a child or adult.

CONNECT WITH OTHERS

2. Which of the following branding slogans would your friends and family say best describes your attitude toward messiness and why?

   ❏ Cleanliness is next to godliness. *(Pears' soap)*

   ❏ It beats as it sweeps as it cleans. *(Hoover vacuum cleaner)*

   ❏ When your shoes shine so do you. *(Kiwi shoe polish)*

   ❏ Don't you just love being in control? *(British Gas)*

   ❏ You deserve a break today. *(McDonalds)*

   ❏ Expanding possibilities ... *(Hewlett Packard)*

   ❏ So much more to enjoy! *(Pepsodent toothpaste)*

   ❏ Fly now. Shovel later. *(Eastern Airlines)*

   ❏ Apparently space isn't the final frontier. *(Syquest)*

NOTE ...

CAPTURE THE LIST ON A VISIBLE FLIP CHART OR POSTER PAGE.

3. As a group, brainstorm about areas of life where we want order but have to accept the truth that they can get messed up.

WHAT'S YOUR STORY?

10-15 MINUTES

In so many ways life is more complicated than we realize. We play a part but we don't always know what part or how it fits with all the others. Is there any chance Goldilocks would have gone into the rustic cabin in the woods if she'd known who lived there? Would Frodo in *The Lord of the Rings* have invited Gandalf into his home if he could have anticipated the sorrow that would follow?

¹ There was a man in the country of Uz named Job. He was a man of perfect integrity, who feared God and turned away from evil. ² He had seven sons and three daughters. ³ His estate included 7,000 sheep, 3,000 camels, 500 yoke of oxen, 500 female donkeys, and a very large number of servants. Job was the greatest man among all the people of the east.

JOB 1:1-3, HCSB

1. Take five minutes **on your own** to write a description of yourself in the style of Job 1:1-3 as if you're the main character in a story. How would you summarize your place in the world, experiences, current relationship with God, and a few facts about yourself that make you unique?

2. Take turns **around the group** reading each self-description. As a group, note any interesting common patterns and distinctions.

"I wonder what kind of tale we've fallen into."

- *Sam and Frodo in The Lord of the Rings*

 INDIVIDUAL EXPERIENCE

- READ JOB 1:1-3 ALOUD
- PROVIDE PAPER AND PENS FOR EACH PERSON
- ALLOW GROUP MEMBERS 5 MINUTES ON THEIR OWN TO WRITE

 **GROUP EXPERIENCE**

- AS A GROUP, DISCUSS SELF-DESCRIPTIONS
- KEEP THIS MOVING AND WATCH YOUR TIME
- IF YOUR GROUP HAS MORE THAN 8 PEOPLE, BREAK INTO SMALLER GROUPS

BEHIND THE SCENES
10-15 MINUTES

CONSIDER THE ➡
LARGER STORY

When e=mc² Doesn't Cut It

The story of Job is not neat and tidy because life can't be boiled down to a set of formulas and equations. Even the messiest of us want and need some constants, some anchors to grab onto when the waves slam into our lives. We systematize, concretize, and homogenize so we can wrap our arms around things and feel some level of control.

NOTE ... ➡

CAPTURE THE LIST ON A VISIBLE FLIP CHART OR POSTER PAGE.

1. What are some the formulas or equations people like to construct about how life works or ought to work? About how God works?

"You get what you have coming."

"Blessing comes with perseverance."

"The patience of Job."

2. What are some of the themes we typically associate with the Book of Job? How about the character lessons we associate with Job?

THEODICY

This theological term refers to the study and defense of God's goodness and justice in light of the evil and suffering in the world.

The most basic interpretation we hear of the Book of Job is that it addresses the age old problem of suffering. All agree that Job helps us better understand why a good God allows suffering.

Yet, for those who desire to take the unfamiliar paths out of their comfort zones, and for those who have eyes to see, the Book of Job has so much more to offer. As we reach beyond just another formula for theodicy, what we discover is a raw, messy, redemptive journey into which God is inviting us.

[Jesus] replied, "You are permitted to understand the secrets of the Kingdom of God. But I use parables to teach the others so that the Scriptures might be fulfilled: 'When they look, they won't really see. When they hear, they won't understand.'"

LUKE 8:10, NLT

3. What is Jesus saying about revealed and hidden truth? How might you apply this to your study of Job's story?

← INTERPRET
← PERSONAL APPLICATION

In *A Sacred Sorrow*, author and singer Michael Card describes the reward of understanding the story of Job and of experiencing disorientation, anguish, and messy searching in your own life. Over time, you'll discover:

Good literature just like all forms of good art guards the deeper secrets for those who will not settle for the superficial or a simplistic formula.

"**The God of the completed equation is a God who is beyond all equations. He is wild and impossible and totally Other. Unknowable. ... But He is also gentle beyond our imagining and available beyond our wildest dreams.**" [1]

UNFOLDING THE LARGER STORY
25-30 MINUTES

In the Book of Job, God pulls back the curtain so we see Job's story—and our own—in the context of the Larger Story, seen and unseen. Just as in classic Greek theatre, the Larger Story plays out in four acts; the first act contains the "once upon a time."

← CONSIDER THE LARGER STORY

Act I: Insurrection in Paradise

God never had a beginning and never has an end, but all the wonders He created had a beginning.

LOGOS

The Greek word *logos* translated "word" could also be "story." *Logos* reveals an idea, tale, or narrative. Jesus is and always has been the "Word" and the "Story."

WITH GOD

The Greek word *pros* indicates much more than presence; it refers to deeply intimate connection.

OBSERVE ➡

In the beginning God created the heavens and the earth.

GENESIS 1:1, HCSB

God: *⁴ Where were you when I established the earth? ... ⁶ On what were its footings set, or who laid its cornerstone—⁷ while the morning stars sang together and all the sons of God shouted for joy?*

JOB 38:4-7, HCSB

¹ In the beginning was the Word, and the Word was with God, and the Word was God. ... ³ All things were created through Him, and apart from Him not one thing was created that has been created.

JOHN 1:1-3, HCSB

1. How do you envision paradise in the heavens and earth "in the beginning"?

⁴ Life was in Him, and that life was the light of men. ⁵ That light shines in the darkness, yet the darkness did not overcome it.

JOHN 1:4-5, HCSB

2. John 1:4 declares that life and light emanated from God. Job 38:7 talks of brilliance, joy, and celebration. What does John 1:5 tell us about the power of "the light" now and its ultimate triumph over darkness?

Heart of Darkness and Betrayal

God created free beings and that by very act brought great risk. Satan, one of God's greatest creations with the heavenly hosts, rose up against his Creator.

14 You were an anointed guardian cherub, for I had appointed you. You were on the holy mountain of God; you walked among the fiery stones. 15 From the day you were created you were blameless in your ways until wickedness was found in you. ... 17 Your heart became proud because of your beauty; For the sake of your splendor you corrupted your wisdom. So I threw you down to the earth.

EZEKIEL 28:14-15,17A, HCSB

12 Shining morning star, how you have fallen from the heavens! You destroyer of nations, you have been cut down to the ground. 13 You said to yourself: "I will ascend to the heavens; I will set up my throne above the stars of God. I will sit on the mount of the gods' assembly, in the remotest parts of the North. 14 I will ascend above the highest clouds; I will make myself like the Most High.

ISAIAH 14:12-14, HCSB

3. According to Isaiah 14 and Ezekiel 28, where did evil originate? What flaws led to the betrayal and insurrection?

4. What happened to the real villain in the Larger Story (Isaiah 14 and Ezekiel 28)? Where does he now reside?

Act II: A Second Beginning and Sabotage

After the first insurrection brought darkness and evil into His brilliant paradise, God took another great risk.

A MASSIVE INSURRECTION

[Satan the dragon:] His tail drew a third of the stars of heaven and threw them to the earth.

- Revelation 12:4, NKJV

The Lord said to Satan, "From where have you come?"

Satan answered the Lord and said, "From going to and fro on the earth, and from walking up and down on it."

- Job 1:6-7, ESV

²⁷ God created man in His own image, in the image of God He created him; male and female He created them. ²⁸ God blessed them and said to them, "Be fruitful and increase in number; fill the earth and subdue it. Rule over the fish of the sea and the birds of the air and over every living creature that moves on the ground." ... ³¹ God saw all that he had made, and it was very good.

GENESIS 1:27-28,31A, NIV

INTERPRET ➡

5. In what sense do men (masculinity) and women (femininity) uniquely reflect aspects of God (verse 27)?

6. According to Genesis 1:28, what did God intend as our ultimate position? What do you think about this?

IMAGO DEI

Unlike every other creation in heaven and earth, we are created in the image of God (*imago dei* in Latin). That is the truest thing about us!

7. What could possibly motivate God to risk another betrayal in giving free will to men and women?

According to Genesis 3, as all heaven watched in horror, we did betray God. Sin entered Eden and our spiritual DNA was contaminated. Satan had struck a deadly and painful blow to God and His beloved.

God speaking to Job: ³¹ Can you bind the chains of the Pleiades, or loose the cords of Orion? ³² Can you bring out Mazzaroth in their season or can you guide the Bear with its children? ³³ Do you know the ordinances of the heavens? Can you establish their rule on the earth?

JOB 38:31-38, ESV

INTERPRET ➡

8. In Job 38, God spells out man's naiveté. Why on earth would God leave Adam and Eve vulnerable to the scheming of His vicious enemy (Genesis 3)?

The villain corrupted the second paradise and we continue to live with the devastating consequences of the attack on God's heirs.

> [20] For the creation was subjected to futility, not willingly, but because of Him who subjected it in hope; [21] because the creation itself also will be delivered from the bondage of corruption into the glorious liberty of the children of God. [23] ... even we ourselves groan within ourselves, eagerly waiting for the adoption, the redemption of our body.
>
> ROMANS 8:20-23, NKJV

Somehow God's sovereignty and man's free choice remain uncompromised in the fall.

Act III: Rescue ... The Tables Are Turned

Far more cunning than Satan, with a plan conceived before time began, Jesus completely turns the tables on His nemesis, rescuing His beloved from despair and captivity. Our Hero risked it all so He could win us back forever!

> [7] No, we speak of God's secret wisdom, a wisdom that has been hidden and that God destined for our glory before time began. [8] None of the rulers of this age understood it, for if they had, they would not have crucified the Lord of glory.
>
> 1 CORINTHIANS 2:7-8, NIV

9. First Corinthians 2:6-8 shows cunning in God's redemptive plan. In what ways does the gospel story demonstrate this from beginning to end?

God knows that with freedom comes risk. Even in betrayal, He stood ready with the secret plan of redemption that his enemy could never have anticipated and would forever regret enacting.

> [12] But our High Priest [Jesus] offered himself to God as a single sacrifice for sins, good for all time. Then he sat down in the place of honor at God's right hand. [13] There he waits until his enemies are humbled and made a footstool under his feet. [14] For by that one offering he forever made perfect those who are being made holy.
>
> HEBREWS 10:12-14, NLT

10. According to Hebrews 10:12-14, what part of Jesus' rescue is complete? Do you think our Priest and King is waiting passively?

"Everything my heart desires Lord, I want it all to be for You, Jesus. Be my magnificent obsession."

- *"Magnificent Obsession"* written and performed by Steven Curtis Chapman

Act IV: Eden Restored

We have been rescued, but we still live in a world where redemption has not been fully realized. Our hearts still long for Eden. Thankfully, the story God is writing will end with a "happily ever after"!

> ²² *So also, golden splendor comes from the mountain of God. He is clothed in dazzling splendor.* ²³ *We cannot imagine the power of the Almighty; but even though he is just and righteous, he does not destroy us.*
>
> **JOB 37:22-23, NLT**

> ¹⁰ *The day of the Lord will come like a thief. The heavens will disappear with a roar; the elements will be destroyed by fire, and the earth and everything in it will be laid bare. ...*
> ¹² *... That day will bring about the destruction of the heavens by fire, and the elements will melt in the heat.* ¹³ *But in keeping with his promise we are looking forward to a new heaven and a new earth, the home of righteousness.*
>
> **2 PETER 3:10-13, NIV**

Thank God He's not who we think He is.

"Papa reached for the kitchen timer, gave it a twist, and placed it in front of them. 'I'm not who you think I am, MacKenzie.' Her words weren't angry or defensive."

- From The Shack by William P. Young

11. Why do you think God restrains His justice and holiness from wiping out a fallen world? Elaborate Job 37:22-23 and other ideas you have.

The Day of the Lord described in Job 37 and 2 Peter 3 will be utterly terrifying to those who do not place their hearts and trust in Jesus alone.

PERSONAL APPLICATION ➡

12. Why do Christ-followers have nothing to fear?

THE HEARTBEAT OF THE STORY

10-15 MINUTES

We are living in the heated battleground of Act III of the Larger Story. Your heart is the prize. The enemy is real and uses live ammunition.

But we live in victory and hope as we wait for our redemption to be fully realized when Jesus returns in "golden splendor from the mountain of God."

1. How have you been personally affected by looking at Job and reviewing the Larger Story?

2. Are there struggles and messes in which you're engaged? If so, talk about them and how can this group encourage you to stay in the fight.

Worship and Prayer Requests

Respond in prayer to God's ancientness and eternal cunning for which no created angel (Lucifer) is any match.

Thank Him for:
   (1) The freedom He has given us
   (2) The risk He's taken
   (3) Ultimately making a way back for us.

Notes:

1. Michael Card, *A Sacred Sorrow* (Colorado Springs, CO: NavPress, 2005), p. 45.

CONNECT WITH OTHERS, WITH GOD, AND WITH YOUR OWN HEART.

TAKE A LITTLE EXTRA TIME TO GO OVER THE GROUP COVENANT (PAGE 123).

PASS AROUND YOUR BOOKS TO COLLECT CONTACT INFO IN THE GROUP DIRECTORY (PAGE 128).

 **CONNECT WITH OTHERS**

 **CONNECT WITH GOD**

TAKE-HOME ACTIVITIES:

• THE "REFLECTION" AND "EXPERIENCE" SECTIONS ARE POWERFUL.

• THE "EXTRA STUDY" SECTION ENCOURAGES YOU TO READ ABOUT THE UNSEEN REALITY.

CONNECTING WITH MY STORY THIS WEEK

EXPERIENCE
TIMES OF PAIN

Between now and your next group session, read chapters 1–3 of the Book of Job. Find a quiet place where you can focus and try to read this in one sitting. As you read …

- Keep a list of specific painful events and difficult circumstances in your life.

- Note any indications, as you look back, of ways that God may have just turned the tables on the enemy and redeemed these times in your life or to help others.

- Identify any unresolved questions or issues business you have for or with God related to these tough times.

REFLECTION – QUESTIONS TO TAKE TO MY HEART AND GOD

After your "Experience" activity, take some time to grapple with what drives your thinking and behavior. Our behaviors are the best indicators of what we really believe in our heart of hearts. Seek to understand what you really believe in your innermost being (Psalm 51:6, NASB) about God, yourself, and the world in which you live.

- Why do my actions, habits, or reactions to painful or difficult seasons in my life reveal about my core beliefs about God or the story I'm in?

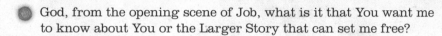

Now, it's time to ask God a question. Be careful not to rush or manufacture an answer. Don't write down what you think the "right" answer is. Don't turn the Bible into a reference book or spiritual encyclopedia. Just pose a question to God and wait for Him. Anything God speaks will always be consistent with the Scripture. Be sure to write down what you hear from God.

> God, from the opening scene of Job, what is it that You want me to know about You or the Larger Story that can set me free?

EXTRA STUDY
TWO INTERSECTING REALITIES

You might want to do additional Bible study on your own. Don't let this "Extra Study" distract you from time spent in the "Experience" and "Reflection" activities.

As God pulls back the curtain on the spiritual realm, we see glimpses of this parallel reality. As you read these Scriptures, jot down notes, thoughts, and feelings.

Luke 8:26-39; John 17:9-18; Romans 8; 1 Corinthians 15:20-50; 2 Corinthians 4:16-18; 10:3-5; Ephesians 6:10-18

DANGEROUS ADVENTURES

AN EPIC ROMANCE

VILLAINS & MONSTERS TO BE SLAIN

A BEAUTY TO BE RESCUED

BETRAYAL & INTRIGUE

BATTLES TO BE FOUGHT AND WON

UNEXPECTED TWISTS & TURNS

GOOD ULTIMATELY TRIUMPHS OVER EVIL

A HERO-REDEEMER

PARADISE RESTORED

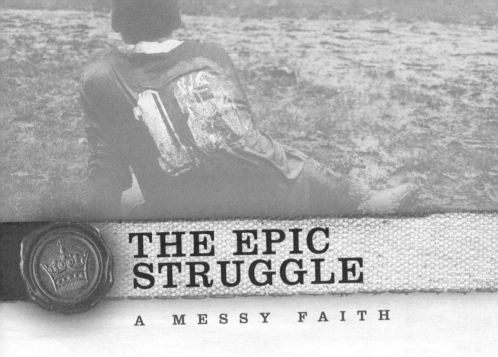

THE EPIC STRUGGLE

A MESSY FAITH

[Satan said:] "Have you not put a hedge around [Job] and his house and all that he has, on every side? ... But stretch out your hand and touch all that he has, and he will curse you to your face."

JOB 1:10-11, ESV

Suddenly a mighty wind swept in from the desert and struck the four corners of the house. It collapsed on them and they are dead, and I am the only one who has escaped to tell you!"

JOB 1:19, NIV

LARGER STORY SYNOPSIS

Our individual stories—our lives—can seem random. But the truth is that we're entangled in a story much larger than our individual stories.

There is a much greater reality beyond what we see and touch in our daily lives. It can either be scary or inspiring to think that we're part of a larger, unpredictable, unseen story. Occasionally we catch glimpses of a backstory or foreshadowings of a future story. It feels like something must connect these glimpses and every individual's experiences into the most complex novel ever written. Job's story is one chapter in this meganovel in which God pulls back the curtain to reveal *the* epic struggle.

OPENING SCENE

10-15 MINUTES

THREE VOLUNTEERS SHOULD READ ASAPH'S DRAMATIC MONOLOGUE ALOUD.

Asaph was a prominent priest and one of King David's three chief musicians. With the help of his sons and others, Asaph was the chief conductor for the great chorus (1 Chronicles 25) and for the dedication of the temple (2 Chronicles 5). He wrote the heartfelt Psalms 50 and 73-82.

Can We Talk?

My name is Asaph. I'm a Levite in King David's service. I'm one of the wise men of Israel, a writer of Psalms and wisdom. We often say things like, "Blessings are on the head of the righteous." [1] I know it's generally true but, as for me, I nearly lost it altogether.[2] I can't talk to my colleagues; I have to keep this to myself. I've always believed in God's wisdom, but doubts are creeping in.

We teach the principle that blessing is God's way for the righteous and that the wicked will be cursed. Yet I've seen the wicked prosper and I've even envied the arrogant.[3] I live the poor life of a priest and scholar, but I know many who have so much more in this world. They have an easy time until they die.[4] Pride is their necklace and they even dare to set their mouths against heaven.[5] Have I lived a pure and godly life for nothing?[6]

I am afflicted all day long.[7] Life has not been good of late. I don't have everything I need. Meanwhile, these who don't honor God live at ease and increase their wealth.[8] Who can really understand the ways of God with men? Why is He silent?

1. Proverbs 10:6; 2. Psalm 73:2; 3. Psalm 73:3; 4. Psalm 73:4; 5. Psalm 73:6,9; 6. Psalm 73:13; 7. Psalm 73:14; 8. Psalm 73:12

PERSONAL ➡ APPLICATION

1. What in Asaph's story reminds you of your own struggles in sorting out life, success, and godliness? In what ways can you relate to Asaph?

Asaph lived in the time of David, and Job probably lived around the time of Abraham. The problem of suffering and why God allows it is not a new discussion; it's an ancient question that has plagued people from the beginning of time.

2. How often do you see godly people (yourself included) suffering and godless people prospering? How has this problem affected your faith in God?

◀ CONNECT WITH
YOUR HEART

3. How do think God feels about our suffering? How do you think He feels if we complain and lament the way Asaph did in the monologue?

◀ INTERPRET

WHAT'S YOUR STORY?
5-10 MINUTES

◀ HOW YOUR
INDIVIDUAL STORY FITS
INTO THE LARGER STORY

As you spent some time this past week with your heart and God, what one insight about the Larger Story or the messiness of life captured your focus?

BEHIND THE SCENES
15-20 MINUTES

Through the Looking Glass

Just as Alice found Wonderland by stepping through the looking glass and four children found Narnia by stepping through a wardrobe, Neo (Keanu Reeves) in the blockbuster film, *The Matrix*, came to recognize an unseen reality he'd never known. Once he accepted the truth of the Matrix, his life was never the same again.

◀ GROUP EXPERIENCE
• READ ALOUD THE "THROUGH THE LOOKING GLASS" PARAGRAPH
• PREP THE DVD PLAYER TO SHOW A CLIP FROM *THE MATRIX* (1999)

GROUP EXPERIENCE CONT'D

• SHOW SCENES 8, "MORPHEUS'
PROPOSAL," AND 9, "DOWN
THE RABBIT HOLE" (FROM
25:07 TO 28:49 MINUTES ON
DVD TIMER)

• END AFTER MORPHEUS PULLS
OUT A PILLBOX AND SAYS,
"NO ONE CAN BE TOLD WHAT
THE MATRIX IS …"

• DISCUSS QUESTIONS 1-2.

1. What's the concept in *The Matrix* of life on two levels? How did Neo (Keanu Reeves) come to realize that there was an unseen reality beyond what he could experience with his five senses?

Morpheus refers to life in the Matrix as being "born into a prison you cannot smell or taste or touch." A limited view of reality is like a prison cell, reducing our perspective to the confines of the cell.

2. What in our reality corresponds to the Matrix? What are some effects as billions of people are born into *our* Matrix, never knowing anything beyond it?

GROUP EXPERIENCE:
PART 2

• ASK A VOLUNTEER
TO READ ALOUD THE
"PULLING BACK THE
CURTAIN" PARAGRAPH

• SHOW A SECOND CLIP
FROM THE MATRIX (1999)

• SCENE 12, "THE REAL
WORLD" BEGINS AT 38:39
MINUTES ON
THE DVD TIMER

• END MID-SCENE (41:18
MINUTES ON THE TIMER)

• DISCUSS QUESTIONS 3-5

Pulling Back the Curtain

After Neo learns there are actually two parallel realities, Morpheus and the others extract Neo from the Matrix and he joins the real world. Neo, like anyone stepping into a whole new mind-set, struggles with truth and old perceptions of reality.

3. How would you answer the question Morpheus poses: "What is real? How do *you* define real?"

4. Consider the Larger Story and the unseen reality revealed in Job. What is our parallel to the "real world" Neo is beginning to see? How many people see it?

Later in *The Matrix* a guy named Cypher makes a deal with the enemy to get himself reinserted back into the blissful ignorance of the Matrix.

5. Discuss whether people would rather be like Neo who knows the terrible truth of the Matrix or like Cypher, blissfully ignorant of the dangers of the unseen reality? Why might people choose the Matrix?

There are times when our stories are confusing, difficult, or deeply painful and overwhelming. A movie like *The Matrix* raises questions like, *"What's the reality behind the scenes that holds all our experiences together and gives them meaning?"* ... *"Is this all there is to life?"* ... and *"Why is this happening to me?!"*

Like most of the people in the world of the Matrix, Job spent much of his life either unaware or disinterested in the Large Story.

 # UNFOLDING THE LARGER STORY

25-30 MINUTES

Although the essential plot of the story occurs in chapters 1–2 and 42, Job is a long book about one chapter in Job's life. The story of the world would yield a monumental collection of books, overflowing all of the world's libraries. No one could possibly write the story or understand the connections except God who sees all.

The Drama in Heaven

Job ... the lone protagonist, unaware of the Grand Stage and the epic struggle. The drama in the heavens shapes events on earth.

"I know why you're here, Neo. I know what you've been doing ... why you hardly sleep, why you live alone, and why night after night, you sit by your computer. ... I was looking for an answer. It's the question that drives us, Neo. It's the question that brought you here."

- *Trinity from* The Matrix

ACCUSER

Especially in the Old Testament, one of Satan's names or titles is the "Accuser." The Accuser calls out complaints against God's people in the heavenly court.

OBSERVE ➤

INTERPRET ➤

<u>Neo:</u> "What is the Matrix?"

<u>Trinity:</u> "The answer is out there, Neo, and it's looking for you, and it will find you if you want it to."

- *From* The Matrix

⁶ One day the sons of God came to present themselves before the LORD, and Satan, the Accuser, came with them. ⁷ "Where have you come from?" the LORD asked Satan. "I have been patrolling the earth, watching everything that's going on."

JOB 1:6-7, NLT

⁴ Where were you when I established the earth? Tell Me, if you have understanding. ... ⁷ while the morning stars sang together and all the sons of God shouted for joy?

JOB 38:4,7, HCSB

1. From your reading of Job 1 and 38, who are the "sons of God"? How are they similar to Satan? How are they different?

2. What kind of access does Satan have on the earth? Why would God's adversary show up in the heavenly council after patrolling the earth?

From these and other Bible passages, we recognize that the "morning stars" and "sons of God" are the ancients in the spiritual realm, predating the creation of mankind. Satan, once amongst them, still has access to God.

⁸ And the Lord said to Satan, "Have you considered my servant Job, that there is none like him on the earth, a blameless and upright man, who fears God and turns away from evil?"

⁹ Then Satan answered the Lord and said, "Does Job fear God for no reason? ¹⁰ Have you not put a hedge around him and his house and all that he has, on every side? You have blessed the work of his hands, and his possessions have increased in the land. ¹¹ But stretch out your hand and touch all that he has, and he will curse you to your face."

Job is most
affected by the
drama in the
heavens, but
knows least about
what's going on.

*12 And the Lord said to Satan, "Behold, all
that he has is in your hand. Only against him
do not stretch out your hand." So Satan went
out from the presence of the Lord.*

JOB 1:8-12, ESV

3. What do you make of God having an intimate,
detailed awareness of Job's life?

4. Is God picking a fight with the Accuser, using
Job as His bait or target?

← INTERPRET

5. Think about your own life and walk with God.
Although we all have issues, why might God
point *you* out to His archenemy?

← PERSONAL
APPLICATION

6. How would you rephrase or characterize the
essence of Satan's accusation in verses 9-11
about God and His relationship with Job?

WE'LL DELVE DEEPER
INTO THIS ACCUSATION
IN A LATER SESSION.

The Shock Waves on Earth

*MESSENGER 1: 13 One day when Job's sons and
daughters were feasting and drinking wine at
the oldest brother's house, 14 a messenger came
to Job and said, "The oxen were plowing and
the donkeys were grazing nearby, 15 and the
Sabeans attacked and carried them off. They put
the servants to the sword, and I am the only one
who has escaped to tell you!"*

INVITE FOUR DIFFERENT
PEOPLE TO READ EACH
OF THESE MESSAGES.

God allows the painful mystery of Job to unfold.

MESSENGER 2: [16] *While he was still speaking, another messenger came and said, "The fire of God fell from the sky and burned up the sheep and the servants, and I am the only one who has escaped to tell you!"*

MESSENGER 3: [17] *While he was still speaking, another messenger came and said, "The Chaldeans formed three raiding parties and swept down on your camels and carried them off. They put the servants to the sword, and I am the only one who has escaped to tell you!"*

MESSENGER 4: [18] *While he was still speaking, yet another messenger came and said, "Your sons and daughters were feasting and drinking wine at the oldest brother's house, [19] when suddenly a mighty wind swept in from the desert and struck the four corners of the house. It collapsed on them and they are dead, and I am the only one who has escaped to tell you!"*

JOB 1:13-19, NIV

OBSERVE ➡

7. God prohibited Satan from laying a hand on Job personally. What areas did he attack? What do you think about the complexity, power, and effectiveness displayed in his strategy?

PERSONAL ➡
APPLICATION

8. If comparable tragedies happened to you, how do you think you'd react? What are some of the reasons people use to explain why tragic things happen in their lives?

Some things that happen in out lives have nothing to do with us

Do We Really Matter?

In Session 1, we discussed the Larger Story into which we were born. In this session, we've begun to piece together the profound implications of this Larger Story on our lives.

As we consider its massive scope, it's no surprise that we, like Job, doubt that we really matter at all. In Psalm 8 and 139, David expresses this same deep question of the heart and is amazed at God's answer.

> *³ When I observe Your heavens, the work of Your fingers, the moon and the stars, which You set in place, ⁴ what is man that You remember him, the son of man that You look after him? ⁵ You made him little less than God and crowned him with glory and honor. ⁶ You made him lord over the works of Your hands; You put everything under his feet.*
>
> **PSALM 8:3-6, HCSB**

> *¹³ For it was You who created my inward parts; You knit me together in my mother's womb. ¹⁴ I will praise You, because I have been remarkably and wonderfully made. ... ¹⁶ Your eyes saw me when I was formless; all my days were written in Your book and planned before a single one of them began.*
>
> **PSALM 139:13-16, HCSB**

9. What do Psalm 8 and 139 reveal about the wonder and glory of mankind as well as each individual? As you let these statements settle into your heart and soul, does anything surprise you?

 PERSONAL APPLICATION

10. Given Psalm 8 and 139 and what we've read of Job's story so far, do you think Job really matters to God? What about us? How and why are we significant to God?

"Who am I, that the Lord of all the earth would care to know my name, would care to feel my hurt."

- "Who Am I?" by Mark Hall; performed by Casting Crowns

INTERPRET ➡

11. In the scheme of world events, how important was Job's tragedy? On the other hand, how significant would you say Job's tragedy and response was to the Larger Story and epic struggle between God and Satan?

We have no way of seeing the heavenly and earthly ripple effects of every event and decision in our lives. Only God sees this massive, complex picture.

Job was in a story far bigger than he ever realized. The size of the story alone makes us doubt that we matter. As we continue in Job's story, we'll see that he did have significant doubts. And he couldn't have been more wrong!

Discounting all the other spiritual and earthly ripple effects of Job's story, just the record of his suffering and glimpses into the unseen realms have helped amazing numbers of people for centuries.

THE HEARTBEAT OF THE STORY
10-15 MINUTES

A Place in the Larger Story

CONSIDER THE LARGER STORY ➡

- HELP OTHER GROUP MEMBERS BEGIN TO CONNECT WITH THEIR OWN STORIES.

- ENCOURAGE EVERYONE KNOW THIS GROUP IS A SAFE PLACE TO BE OPEN AND REAL.

Job's choices seem small but loom large in the epic struggle. More than that, Job himself matters in a big way just for the role he plays as the beloved, the wrestler, the friend of God. And others matter because each one has been called to a unique role alongside the Hero-Redeemer, Jesus. Our role might include the waiting with anticipation in part of the beauty to be rescued and joining Jesus in His redemptive mission.

Jesus speaking to His followers: [6] *What is the price of five sparrows—two copper coins? Yet God does not forget a single one of them.* [7] *And the very hairs on your head are all numbered. So don't be afraid; you are more valuable to God than a whole flock of sparrows.*

LUKE 12:6-7, NLT

God speaking to His chosen people and by extension to us: Do not fear, for I have redeemed you; I have called you by your name; you are Mine.

ISAIAH 43:1B; 45:4, HCSB

1. In Luke 12, Jesus assures us of our value to God and His deep care for us. We know Jesus died to save us, but in what personal ways has God expressed His love and appreciation for you?

2. In Isaiah 43:4, God emphasizes: "I have called you by your name." What's the significance of this to us?

3. Think about your current challenges and difficulties. How does accepting that you're not the central figure in the story—that it's not all about you—affect the way you approach life?

4. How do you feel knowing that God knows you intimately and cares deeply about you?

God alone sees the big picture while we're stuck within the story. Yet God doesn't just watch from above—He fully engages in all the subplots of the story.

◄ **CONNECT WITH YOUR HEART**

"Be kind, for everyone you meet is fighting a great battle."
- *Philo of Alexandria*

 CONNECT WITH GOD

We might summarize God's message like this:

"I am the Maker and the Redeemer. I know all
and you know only part. Trust Me—I've ensured
ultimate victory on the Grand Stage. Your part
in the story may be hard to understand, but it's
eternally significant. The results of the subplots
and scenes you're involved in are uncertain and
at risk! Trust Me—I know the outcomes, even the
painful ones and how they fit together in eternity.

"You may perform many big and small acts of
heroism in your lifetime. Or you may not use
what I've given you. I leave that for you to decide."

Worship and Prayer Requests

Spend a few minutes in quiet personal prayer.

Acknowledge that it's not all about you.

Accept that some things that happen have nothing
to do with us—right or wrong.

Thank God that circumstances are no indicator of
His love or approval.

Record group prayer requests and struggles. Pray
regularly for each between now and the next session.

TAKE-HOME ACTIVITIES:

• THE "REFLECTION" AND
"EXPERIENCE" SECTIONS
ARE POWERFUL

• THE "EXTRA STUDY"
SECTION PROVIDES
SOLID PREWORK ON
SATAN FOR SESSION 3

CONNECTING WITH MY STORY THIS WEEK

EXPERIENCE
BEGIN TO OPEN UP

Our lives are often so hurried that we don't make the time we need to connect personally with God. He longs to meet with us and to hear our joys, our worries, and even our complaints or accusations. Find a place where you can be alone with God and make an effort to pour out what's really in your heart.

REFLECTION – QUESTIONS TO TAKE TO MY HEART AND GOD

After your "Experience," take some time for introspection to discover what drives your thinking and behavior. Your behaviors are the best indicator of what you really believe in our innermost being (Psalm 51:6, NASB) about God, yourself, and the world in which you live.

- Being brutally honest, in what ways have I lived as though the story is all about me? What beliefs have I carried that have fueled my response to blessings and suffering?

Now, it's time to ask God a question. Just pose the question and wait. Anything God speaks will always be consistent with the Scripture.

- God, I'm far from perfect and my life is messy, but what is there about me that makes You proud? What gifts or weapons have You given me that make me dangerous to the enemy?

EXTRA STUDY
SATAN AND ANGELS

As God pulls back the curtain on the spiritual realm, we see glimpses of the backstory. A study of Satan and angels could fill several volumes and still be incomplete because much of the spiritual realm is still a mystery. The following topics and verses will give you a somewhat clearer picture of both Satan and the angels.

As you have time, look at each of the Scriptures listed and jot down notes and thoughts related to each subtopic.

The Serpent
Genesis 3:1-7; 2 Corinthians 11:3; Revelation 12:9

The Serpent's plan in the Garden of Eden:

The Serpent's potential effect on me:

The identity of the Serpent revealed:

Angels and Creation
Job 38:4-7; Psalm 8; Psalm 103:19-22

Angels in time relationship to people:

Angels in time relationship to Creation:

Angels as morning stars; their glory compared to people:

Angels compared to God:

Angels as Ministering Spirits
Daniel 9:21-23; Acts 8:26; Psalm 34:4-7; Psalm 91:9-16; Hebrews 1:13-14; Matthew 13:37-42

God's role or commission for angels:

Power of angels:

Involvement in judgment of the wicked:

Origin of Evil ... The Morning Star Cast Down
Isaiah 14:12-15; Job 38:7

NOTE: In Isaiah 14:12, the NIV and HCSB use "morning star;" ESV and NRSV use "Day Star;" NKJV uses "Lucifer;" and NLT uses "shining star."

Possible correlation between Job 38:7 and Isaiah 14:12:

The story of the morning star (Satan):

Cherub in Eden
Genesis 3:1,24; Ezekiel 28:12-17

CHERUB: Guardian angel; guarded the way back to Eden in Genesis 3:24; guarded God's holiness above the Ark in Exodus 25:22; four cherubim surrounding the throne of God in Ezekiel 10 and Revelation 4.

Possible correlation of Ezekiel 28:13 and Genesis 3:1:

The story of the Cherub and the Cherubim in Eden:

Satan's Dominion
Job 1:7; 2:2; 1 Peter 5:8

Possible correlation of Job 1:7; 2:2; and 1 Peter 5:8:

Purpose of Satan's ranging to and fro:

DANGEROUS ADVENTURES

AN EPIC ROMANCE

VILLAINS & MONSTERS TO BE SLAIN A BEAUTY TO BE RESCUED

BETRAYAL & INTRIGUE

BATTLES TO BE FOUGHT

AND WON UNEXPECTED TWISTS & TURNS

GOOD ULTIMATELY TRIUMPHS OVER EVIL

A HERO-REDEEMER

PARADISE

RESTORED

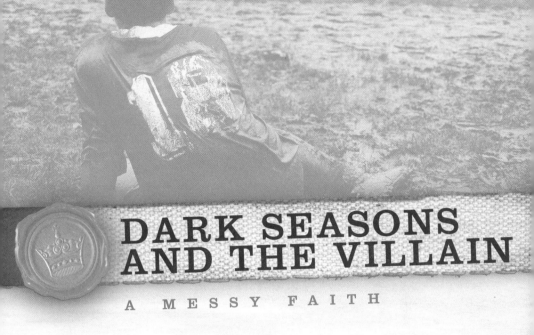

DARK SEASONS AND THE VILLAIN

A M E S S Y F A I T H

So Satan left the LORD's presence and infected Job with incurable boils from the sole of his foot to the top of his head.

JOB 2:7, HCSB

Then Job answered: "How long will you torment me and crush me with words? You have humiliated me ten times now, and you mistreat me without shame.

JOB 19:1-3, HCSB

LARGER STORY SYNOPSIS

Good will ultimately triumph over evil; God will reign undisputed as King of kings and Lord of lords. But for now evil still holds sway, unleashing pain and destruction.

Many stories have villains who work against all that is good in the lives of the other characters. The stories we enjoy mirror the reality of the Larger Story—the reality about God, us, and how we got where we are. There is a desperate and savage villain in the story who can and does win in many subplots of the Larger Story. Evil seems to rule the day as we experience pain, suffering, shattered dreams, and destruction all around us, yet often we minimize the villain's role or impact in our stories.

CONNECT WITH ➡
OTHERS

- EASE IN WITH LIGHTHEARTED DISCUSSION

- CONTINUE TO SHARE YOUR STORIES

OPENING SCENE

10-15 MINUTES

1. My life is most like ...

   ❏ An uphill race—I'm always behind and I can't catch up.
   ❏ An air-conditioned igloo—It seems pointless.
   ❏ Drying paint—It's so boring I think watching paint dry would be an improvement.
   ❏ An amusement park—I guess I should feel guilty about all the fun I'm having.
   ❏ A newly frozen pond—I'm skating on thin ice and I pray it holds.
   ❏ A bowl of cherries—I haven't chomped down on a cherry pit for a while.
   ❏ A reality show—It's not always entertaining, but it is real.

Why did you say that?

Consider epic stories like *The Lord of the Rings, The Chronicles of Narnia, Star Wars,* and *Sleeping Beauty*. There are always villains and, often, archvillains controlling the forces of evil from the top.

2. Who are the villains and archvillains in the stories you love? What can happen when villains work undetected in secret and largely unchallenged?

"Well I'm gaining power by the hour. They're falling by the score. You know, it's getting very easy now since no one believes in me anymore."

- *"No One Believes In Me Anymore"* by Keith Green

3. Why would it be critical for us to acknowledge the villain and assign blame accurately in the Larger Story and in our lives?

WHAT'S YOUR STORY?

5-10 MINUTES

1. As you spent time this week in reflection and prayer, what did God reveal to you about your value to Him and your role in the Larger Story?

← HOW YOUR INDIVIDUAL STORY FITS INTO THE LARGER STORY

2. Were there any surprises as you studied the serpent, angels, morning star, cherub in Eden, and Satan as a roaming lion? Share your thoughts or feelings with the group.

← OPTIONAL ... IF TIME ALLOWS

BEHIND THE SCENES

10-15 MINUTES

1. How largely does Satan figure into your view of the world and daily interpretation of your life?

> Theology is not just theory, and the Bible's stories are not whimsical accounts. The unseen reality deeply affects our lives.

SATAN'S RESUME

A.K.A. Beelzebub, the Adversary, Prince of the Power of the Air, the Devil, the Strongman, the Accuser, the Serpent, and the Father of Lies.

MY OBJECTIVE

To capture the throne of God or at least as much power as possible; to avenge previous humiliation; to hurt God at every opportunity; to ruin for others the good now unavailable to me and bring others down with me.

TAKE TURNS READING PARTS OF SATAN'S RESUME ALOUD TO THE GROUP.

Continued ...

BACKGROUND

- One of the morning stars/angels created by God with other heavenly hosts before man's creation (Job 38:7)

- Source of the knowledge of evil in the human story (Genesis 3)

- Appeared as the serpent in Eden (2 Corinthians 11:3; Revelation 12:9; 20:2)

FORMER EMPLOYMENT

- Perfect and beautiful guardian angel (cherub) in Paradise (Ezekiel 28:12-17)

- Leader of the insurrection when more than a third of heaven rebelled against God (Isaiah 14:13; Revelation 12:4,9)

- Murderer: from early on developed a jealous and murderous heart (John 8:44)

- Adversary and tempter Jesus Christ, God's Anointed (Matthew 4:1-11)

STRONG POINTS

- **Agenda Setter:** Influential in directing this world's value system (John 12:31; Ephesians 2:2; Matthew 4:8-9; 2 Corinthians 4:4)

- **Destructive:** Seeking to devour and sift souls (1 Peter 5:8; Luke 22:31)

- **Supervision:** Organize unseen earth patrols (Job 1:7; 2:2)

- **Great Tempter:** Source of outside temptation for humans, adding to their own internal distortions (1 Thessalonians 3:5; Corinthians 2:11)

- **Cunning:** Effective in blinding the spiritual eyes of non-believers (2 Corinthians 4:3-4)

- **Malicious:** Oppressing and possessing vulnerable people (John 13:27)

- **Persistent:** Afflicting God's servants (Luke 22:31; 1 Thessalonians 2:18)

- **Master Deceiver:** Deceiving and lying to achieve my ends (John 8:44)

- **Stubborn:** Unwilling servant of God (1 Chronicles 21:1; compare 2 Samuel 24:1)

To live in truth and strength, we must accept the reality of the unseen villain whose treachery is behind much of our human struggle, just as in Job's life.

The "Strongman is not allowed to oppress Christ-followers at will.

2. Compare Satan to the great villains from other stories: The Emperor (*Star Wars*,) Commodus (*Gladiator*), Sauron (*The Lord of the Rings*), the White Witch (*The Chronicles of Narnia*), Malefocent (*Sleeping Beauty*), and so on.

◀ INTERPRET

3. After reading through Satan's resume, how did it affect you?

◀ CONNECT WITH
YOUR HEART

4. How and why do you think the "ruler of this world" stays essentially hidden and unacknowledged in our lives?

The problem with not recognizing and understanding the villain in the Larger Story and our stories is that we end up blaming the wrong people.

- If we blame God, we become disillusioned.

- If we blame others, we villainize people.

UNFOLDING THE LARGER STORY

25-30 MINUTES

The Villain's Fury and Fate

If we're going to make sense of life, we must grasp the intent of the villain and learn to recognize the evil tactics he employs behind the scenes in our lives. We discussed in Session 1 that Satan was a wonderful, perfect creation of God until his pride and wickedness corrupted him and many others. He conceived evil from his heart, he lives in total rebellion to God, and his ultimate fate is sealed.

> [12] *You were the seal of perfection, full of wisdom and perfect in beauty.* [13] *You were in Eden, the garden of God. Every kind of precious stone covered you .... Your mountings and settings were crafted in gold.* [17] *... For the sake of your splendor you corrupted your wisdom. So I threw you down to the earth; I made a spectacle of you before kings.*
>
> **EZEKIEL 28:12B-13,17, HCSB**

> [12] *Shining morning star, how you have fallen from the heavens! You destroyer of nations, you have been cut down to the ground. ...*
> [15] *But you will be brought down to Sheol into the deepest regions of the Pit.*
>
> ***ISAIAH 14:12,15, HCSB***

> *The Devil who deceived them was thrown into the lake of fire and sulfur ... and they will be tormented day and night forever and ever.*
>
> ***REVELATION 20:10, HCSB***

CONNECT WITH ➡️

1. Applying these words from Ezekiel, Isaiah, and Revelation to Satan, how do you suppose he felt and still feels about God after God cut him down, made a spectacle of him among the heavenly hosts, and sealed his destruction?

2. How do you think Satan feels about God's creation, and especially that creation made in God's image (*imago dei*)?

Satan learned long ago that he cannot win a direct assault against God. However, God is exposed because of giving man freedom of choice. Satan tries to exploit that vulnerability.

3. If you were on the side of evil, how would you "get to" God in a way that would actually hurt Him? How could you cause Father, Son, and Holy Spirit the most grief and pain possible while striving to avoid your impending doom?

Frontal Assault on Job

We read in Session 2 how Job received four devastating blows in rapid succession in the first waves of assaults by Satan and those he influence. The words used to describe the attacks in Job 1:13-19 reveal insights about the villain we face.

- "Attacked ... put to the sword"
- "Fire of God fell from the sky"
- "Raiding parties swept down ... put to the sword"
- "Mighty wind struck ... collapsed ... dead"

> *Be sober! Be on the alert! Your adversary the Devil is prowling around like a roaring lion, looking for anyone he can devour.*
>
> **1 PETER 5:8, HCSB**

> [10] *Finally, be strong in the Lord and in his mighty power.* [11] *Put on the full armor of God so that you can take your stand against the devil's schemes.*
>
> **EPHESIANS 6:10-11, NIV**

SATAN

This name used for the villain in Job means "adversary." As such, his chief role is opposing God, His plans, and His people.

4. What do we learn about Satan's character, power, and battle tactics from Job 1:13-19, 1 Peter 5:8, and Ephesians 6:10-11?

◀ **OBSERVE**

5. How can we withstand the enemy's assaults and the traumatic events in our lives like those Job experienced?

◀ **PERSONAL APPLICATION**

> [4] *"Skin for skin!" Satan answered the LORD. "A man will give up everything he owns in exchange for his life.* [5] *But stretch out Your hand and strike his flesh and bones, and he will surely curse You to Your face."* [6] *"Very well," the LORD told Satan, "he is in your power; only spare his life."* [7] *So Satan left the LORD's presence and infected Job with incurable boils from the sole of his foot to the top of his head.*
>
> **JOB 2:4-7, HCSB**

SKIN FOR SKIN

This term's meaning is debated, but Satan keeps pushing God. He claims that Job will certainly disengage from God if it's his own skin ... "I guarantee he'll turn on You."

6. Why does Satan need permission from God to inflict suffering on a believer/follower (Job 1:12 and 2:6)? Considering the Larger Story, why do you think God allowed Satan's attacks on Job?

Subtle Subterfuge and Manipulation

Some of us live with the death of a dream; others with unfulfilled dreams. Our best work isn't good enough. Our health lets us down. Every advance reminds us a fall is coming. The best people fail us—and we them. That great thing disappoints. We're tempted and fall. Solomon said, "everything is meaningless, a chasing after the wind." If anyone had a right to struggle with frustration and faith, it was Job. And he did—deeply.

> *[11] Three of Job's friends heard of all the trouble that had fallen on him. Each traveled from his own country—Eliphaz from Teman, Bildad from Shuhah, Zophar from Naamath—and went together to Job to keep him company and comfort him. ... [13] Then they sat with him on the ground. Seven days and nights they sat there without saying a word. They could see how rotten he felt, how deeply he was suffering.*
>
> ***JOB 2:11,13, THE MESSAGE***

Job's friends set aside everything to be present and comfort him. They **do** comfort for seven days until Job begins to voice his grief, frustrations, and complaints to God. The very act of lamenting to God along with the nature of Job's complaints are abhorrent to his friends' cautious and formulaic faith. It's almost more than they can bear.

Unlike the image of God his friends carry, Job's God isn't formulaic and predictable.

> *Eliphaz: [7] "Think! Has a truly innocent person ever ended up on the scrap heap? Do genuinely upright people ever lose out in the end? [8] It's my observation that those who plow evil and sow trouble reap evil and trouble.*
>
> ***JOB 4:7-8, THE MESSAGE***

God doesn't have a problem with messiness. We're the only ones that have a problem when faith gets messy.

> *Bildad: [3] Does God pervert justice? Does the Almighty pervert what is right? [4] When your children sinned against him, he gave them over to the penalty of their sin. [5] But if you will look to God and plead with the Almighty, [6] if you are pure and upright, even now he will rouse himself on your behalf and restore you to your rightful place. ... [20] Surely God does not reject a blameless man or strengthen the hands of evildoers.*
>
> ***JOB 8:3-6,20, NIV***

Zophar: [6] *Listen! God is doubtless punishing you far less than you deserve! ...* [20] *the wicked will be blinded. They will have no escape. Their only hope is death.*

JOB 11:6B,20, NLT

7. Is there some truth to what Job's friends believe? What's the general life truth these guys are trying to blindly apply to every situation, including Job's?

← OBSERVE

The verbal attacks on Job continued to intensify. Job fired back.

Job responds to his friends: *"Your platitudes are as valuable as ashes. Your defense is as fragile as a clay pot."*

JOB 13:12, NLT

[1] *Then Job replied:* [2] *"I have heard many things like these; miserable comforters are you all!* [3] *Will your long-winded speeches never end? What ails you that you keep on arguing?*

JOB 16:3, NIV

[1] *Then Job answered:* [2] *"How long will you torment me and crush me with words?* [3] *You have humiliated me ten times now, and you mistreat me without shame."*

JOB 19:1-3, HCSB

8. What do you see in the progression of Job's responses to his friends? How do you think you would respond in Job's place if you were enduring intense physical, emotional, and spiritual pain?

As in Job's situation, some difficult circumstances are simply the result of getting caught in the crossfire or drama in the Larger Story. Job's losses and suffering have zero to do with him, his sins, or his bad choices.

We are quick to tie God's redemption of evil with causation. Be very clear: God does not cause evil. He does not take credit for evil, but He always promises to redeem it

Chapters in Job:

- 2 = frontal assault on Job
- 2 or 3 = Job laments to God
- 30+ = dialog of discouragement
- 5 = God speaks

9. How did Satan use Job's friends to wear him down and disrupt his dialog with God? What do you think the enemy was trying to accomplish in Job's heart and mind?

10. Share a time in your life when you struggled with hopeless, defeat, discouragement, or cynicism. What do you recall believing about God and His heart toward you during this season of your life?

THE HEARTBEAT OF THE STORY
10-15 MINUTES

GROUP ➡ EXPERIENCE:

- SET UP DVD PLAYER TO SHOW A CLIP FROM *SPIDER-MAN 2* (2004)
- READ ALOUD THE "I FINALLY GOT TO HIM!" INTRODUCTION
- SHOW SCENE 30 "JAMESON GETS THE SUIT" AND THE START OF SCENE 31 "PETER'S CONFESSION"
- CLIP RUNS ON THE DVD TIMER FROM 1:08:09 TO 1:10:00 (AFTER PETER WALKS AWAY FROM THE ASSAULT)

I Finally Got to Him!

In the film *Spider-Man 2*, Peter Parker (Tobey Maguire) struggles deeply with the difficulty that comes from being Spider-Man. His true identity and mission are vital in the life of his city. The weight of his responsibilities and the trials of life provide enough strain, but the discouragement and incessant lies assigning him ignoble intentions in the *Daily Bugle* run by J. Jonah Jameson (J.K. Simmons) may be the last straw.

1. How did Jonah Jameson twist the truth about Spider-Man? How do you think Jameson's attitude about crushing Spidey's spirit compares to Satan's mind-set toward us?

2. The face of Jameson's coworker speaks volumes about how good and godly people see Spidey's loss of heart. How did giving up affect Spider-Man personally? How did it affect his involvement in the larger story in New York?

◄━ INTERPRET

Satan is an imitator, not a creator. Evil at its heart is the perversion or twisting of what is good. Illicit sex is a good thing corrupted. Selfishness is only about an inch away from helpfulness.

Key Enemy Tactic 1: Cunning Deception

Our adversary is extremely cunning and persuasive. He convinced a third of the heavenly hosts to rebel against Almighty God. He deceived Adam and Eve into distrusting God and ushered in the fall of man. He continues to disrupt or destroy massive numbers of lives every day.

> *Jesus said: You belong to your father, the devil, and you want to carry out your father's desire. He was a murderer from the beginning, not holding to the truth, for there is no truth in him. When he lies, he speaks his native language, for he is a liar and the father of lies.*
> *JOHN 8:44, NIV*

> 7 *Then war broke out in heaven ... So the great dragon was thrown out—the ancient serpent, who is called the Devil and Satan, the one who deceives the whole world. He was thrown to earth, and his angels with him.*
> *REVELATION 12:7-9, HCSB*

3. The villain has no truth in him; lying is his native tongue and his chief tool is manipulation. At what point in Job's life does Satan incessantly speak lies to him? When are you most susceptible to his lies and twisted half-truths?

Beginning to end, the Larger Story is always about our love affair with Jesus. The Adversary desperately wants to disrupt that love.

"But I fear that, as the serpent deceived Eve by his cunning, your minds may be corrupted from a complete and pure devotion to Christ."

- 2 Corinthians 11:3, HCSB

◄━ CONNECT WITH YOUR HEART

Key Enemy Tactic 2: Isolation

Another favorite tactic of the villain in our stories is to isolate us, wear us down, and drag us to despair. If we lose heart and give up, we are more easily taken out.

> [14] "One should be kind to a fainting [or despairing] friend, but you accuse me without any fear of the Almighty. [15] My brothers, you have proved as unreliable as a seasonal brook. ... [25] What do your criticisms amount to? [26] Do you think your words are convincing when you disregard my cry of desperation?
>
> **JOB 6:14-15,25-26, NLT**

> **Job laments:** [1] My spirit is crushed, and my life is nearly snuffed out. The grave is ready to receive me. [2] I am surrounded by mockers. I watch how bitterly they taunt me.
>
> **JOB 17:1-2, NLT**

> A healthy spirit conquers adversity, but what can you do when the spirit is crushed?
>
> **PROVERBS 18:14, THE MESSAGE**

CONNECT ➡ WITH YOUR HEART

4. What approaches can and does the Adversary use to crush our spirits? Discuss various ways he can hurt you, cause you to lose heart, and take you out of your vital role in the Larger Story.

Battle Prayer

Spend time to identify and pray against the cunning assaults that are being launched into the lives of each member of your group.

Record specific group prayer need and pray regularly between now and the next session.

"Everything that has transpired has done so according to my design. Your friends, up there on the sanctuary moon, are walking into a trap, as is your Rebel fleet."

- The evil emperor in Star Wars VI: Return of the Jedi (1983)

TAKE-HOME ACTIVITIES:

- "REFLECTION" IS EXPANDED SO THERE'S NO "EXPERIENCE" THIS WEEK
- REVIEW THE "EXTRA STUDY" SECTION ONLY IF YOU'VE SPENT AMPLE TIME ON "REFLECTION"

CONNECTING WITH MY STORY THIS WEEK

 ## REFLECTION – QUESTIONS TO TAKE TO MY HEART

Why Bad Things Happen:

1. We're born into a time of war with live ammo and high stakes.
2. There's a villain in the story who is ancient, lives as evil personified, and hates you beyond measure.
3. He's a master at twisting the truth and lies to make us question the goodness of God.
4. His goal is to cause us to doubt the heart of God toward us.
5. He strives to disorient us and distort our view of ourselves.
6. God allows freedom of the will because without freedom true love does not exist.
7. God empowers believers to fend off and ultimately defeat the enemy. We need to be prepared to pick up the resources God provides and fire!

Once we recognize the battle being waged for our hearts and souls, the pain and struggles in our lives come into better focus. The Adversary's distortions keep us out of the glory we were intended to live in and the intimacy God wants us to share with Him.

- Into which pivotal events in my life has the enemy launched arrows and created deeply imbedded wounds?

- What are some of the deceptions and twisted truths that the enemy continues to whisper in my ear as difficulties come? What false beliefs have I accepted?

EXTRA STUDY
TRUE LOVE AND TWISTED LOVE

Israel's Creed of Love: Deuteronomy 6:4-5

The readers of Job were quite familiar with the high calling of love that God desired from His people. Eventually Deuteronomy 6:4-5 became Israel's creed, called the *Shema* (shuh-mah, from the first word of the verse in Hebrew). Later, Jesus would make it part of the creed for His followers as well in Mark 12:29-30.

Meaning of "the Lord is one":

Meaning of "love the Lord your God with all your heart":

Meaning of "with all your soul":

Meaning of "with all your strength":

The Love Before Creation: John 17:24 (see also John 1:1)

Who existed "before the world's foundation"?

The doctrine of the Trinity is the New Testament understanding that God is one being who exists at the same time in three distinct persons: Father, Son, and Spirit. The Father is not the Son. The Son is not the Spirit. Yet Father, Son, and Spirit are all God and God is one.

What is the origin of love (see also 1 John 4:8)?

Love and Honesty: Proverbs 27:5-6; 28:23

Job is part of the wisdom literature of the Bible. Throughout the Ancient Near East, there was a kind of literature about wisdom and practical sense for living. Job is a part of a rich tradition. There is a concept of true love and honesty in the wisdom of Israel.

What relationship between love and honesty does Proverbs 27:5 describe?

What are examples of "wounds of a friend" (27:6)?

What are examples of "kisses of an enemy" (27:6)?

Would it be possible for someone to try and flatter God? Explain:

Would it be possible for someone to please God and give Him joy? Explain:

Lamenting and Prayer: Psalm 13:1,5

Included in Israel's wisdom tradition are many psalms and prayers of lament used throughout the story of Israel.

Would you be comfortable praying Psalm 13:1? Explain.

What's the relationship between verses 5 and 1?

What's the relationship between Psalm 13:1 and Proverbs 27:5?

True Love: 1 Corinthians 13:4-7

The relationship of love and selfishness:

The relationship of love and flattery:

The relationship of love and trust:

DANGEROUS ADVENTURES

AN EPIC ROMANCE

VILLAINS & MONSTERS TO BE SLAIN   A BEAUTY TO BE RESCUED

BETRAYAL & INTRIGUE

BATTLES TO BE FOUGHT AND WON   UNEXPECTED TWISTS & TURNS

GOOD ULTIMATELY TRIUMPHS OVER EVIL

A HERO-REDEEMER

PARADISE RESTORED

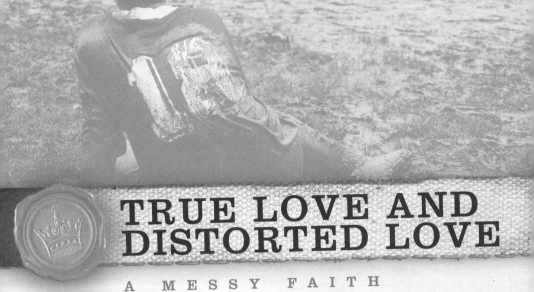

TRUE LOVE AND DISTORTED LOVE

A MESSY FAITH

[Job] fell to the ground and worshiped, saying: "Naked I came from my mother's womb, and naked I will leave this life. The LORD gives, and the LORD takes away. Praise the name of the LORD."

JOB 1:20-21, HCSB

I know that my Redeemer lives, and that in the end he will stand upon the earth. ... I myself will see him with my own eyes—I, and not another. How my heart yearns within me!

JOB 19:25,27, NIV

LARGER STORY SYNOPSIS

A cosmic battle surrounds the Larger Story, but at its core, it's the story of the Epic Romance between a God of pure love and His beloved.

The Larger Story is all about love and romance, from the act of God's creating us to His devotion in restoring us to the beauty we were made to be. Although God doesn't need our love, He wants to be loved as He loves. He delights in the love of His people, but He won't force that love or manipulate it. It must be freely given. In the story of Job, that amazing love shows through. At this exact point the Villain attacks God, trying to corrupt Job's love and rob God's joy in it.

OPENING SCENE
10-15 MINUTES

> "Love can tell, and love alone, whence the million stars are strewn."
>
> *- Robert Bridges*

1. Which modern-day, historical, or fictional couple best exemplifies your ideal of true love? Why does this couple stand out to you?

GROUP EXPERIENCE ➡

- DIVIDE INTO SUBGROUPS OF 3-4 PEOPLE EACH

- USE LARGE SHEETS OF PAPER OR POSTER BOARDS TO CAPTURE EACH SUBGROUP'S IDEAS

2. Within smaller subgroups, take about five minutes to list various characteristics of "true love" and also characteristics of "distorted love."

TRUE OR PURE LOVE	DISTORTED LOVE
1. Honest	1. Fake
2. Passionate	2. Passive
3.	3.
4.	4.
5.	5.
6.	6.
7.	7.
8.	8.
9.	9.
10.	10.

After 5 minutes, pull everyone back together.

3. Gather together as a full group to discuss each subgroup's lists. Highlight those characteristics you see as central to true or pure love.

WHAT'S YOUR STORY?
5-10 MINUTES

HOW YOUR INDIVIDUAL STORY FITS INTO THE LARGER STORY

1. As you have reflected this week on the work of the Villain, did you see areas of evil influence that surprised you?

2. If you spent time with the "Extra Study," what lessons did you learn about love, God, and you?

← OPTIONAL PERSONAL APPLICATION

BEHIND THE SCENES
15-20 MINUTES

John Eldredge writes: "'In the beginning …' before the dawn of time. '… the Word was with God, and the Word was God. He was with God in the beginning.' A fellowship. The Heart of all things. Not a lonely universe, but one born out of Love." [2]

← CONSIDER THE LARGER STORY

No other religion besides the Judeo-Christian faith has love as its central theme. Job is not an explicit story about the Epic Romance between God and His beloved. Yet romance is the story behind the story of the Epic Battle in Job. Look again at the assembly of the heavenly court Job 1–2 within the context of the Epic Romance.

> [8] And the Lord said to Satan, "Have you considered my servant Job, that there is none like him on the earth, a blameless and upright man, who fears God and turns away from evil?" [9] Then Satan answered the Lord and said, "Does Job fear God for no reason? [10] Have you not put a hedge around him and his house and all that he has, on every side? You have blessed the work of his hands, and his possessions have increased in the land. [11] But stretch out your hand and touch all that he has, and he will curse you to your face."
>
> *JOB 1:8-11, ESV*

> [4] "Skin for skin!" Satan answered the LORD. "A man will give up everything he owns in exchange for his life. [5] But stretch out Your hand and strike his flesh and bones, and he will surely curse You to Your face."
>
> *JOB 2:4-5, HCSB*

To love and be loved is the most foundational longing in our human experience. It's who we are because it's who God made us— in His image.

INTERPRET ➡

1. In light of the Epic Romance, why do you think God brings up Job's life and faithfulness to Satan? Given Satan's ultimate fate, why is he even involved in this scene?

INTERPRET ➡

2. In Job 1:11 and 2:5, what accusation or idea is Satan trying to plant in God's mind about Job's love and all God's people? What is he trying to accomplish?

Satan's lie, his poison to attack God's heart, goes like this: "You have to buy their love. They don't really love You for You. They just want Your gifts."

3. Does the reality of Satan working to poison God's heart and ours resonate with your experiences? How does Satan's accusation come into play in your relationship with God?

"Remember when you love, from that same hour your peace you put into your lover's power."

- Anne Killigrew

UNFOLDING THE LARGER STORY

30-35 MINUTES

Distorted Love

As the present ruler of this world, Satan masterminds twisting truth and virtue so that his distortions even seem right to us. The story of Job takes place in the Ancient Near East. Religion in that region was not about love, but about serving gods who were neither omnipotent nor all good. A worshiper's goal was to appease and get blessing from these powerful but unpredictable, capricious gods. This culture clearly influenced Job's friends.

Bildad: [8:6] *If you are pure and upright, even now [God] will rouse himself on your behalf and restore you to your rightful place.* [18:15] *The lamp of the wicked is snuffed out.*

JOB 8:6; 18:15, NIV

2. What is true about God's love in Bildad's comments? What gets twisted or left out as Bildad applies his thinking to Job's situation?

Satan is a liar by nature. By his cunning he mixes some truth with subtle lies to create a blend of hardly discernible deception.

Zophar: [4] *Don't you know that ever since antiquity ...* [5] *the joy of the wicked has been brief and the happiness of the godless has lasted only a moment?*

JOB 20:4-5, HCSB

3. On the surface, Zophar's view of God sounds fair and reasonable. What has he distorted? If God worked according to his formula, how could we reconcile pain and sorrow in our lives?

◀— PERSONAL
APPLICATION

Eliphaz: Can a mortal be more righteous than God? Can a man be more pure than his Maker?

JOB 4:17, NIV

Eliphaz: [15:12] *Why has your heart carried you away, and why do your eyes flash,* [13] *so that you vent your rage against God and pour out such words from your mouth? ...* [25] *he shakes his fist at God and vaunts himself against the Almighty.* [22:21] *Submit to God and be at peace with him ...* [27] *You will pray to him, and he will hear you.*

JOB 15:12-13; 22:21,27, NIV

Job doesn't hold back his feelings as he laments and contends with God. Eliphaz sharply criticizes Job for his rash, transparent approach in expressing his disappointment and disillusionment with God.

4. Does expressing anger, frustration, sorrow to God prevent us from being humble and submissive? How does stuffing our true feelings and guarding our hearts with God lead to a distorted love?

DANGEROUS LIES OF THE VILLAIN:

1. God is too busy for me. I'm not worth His time.
2. He's indifferent and removed.
3. It's up to me to take care of me.
4. God can't even tolerate my messiness and emotions, let alone enjoy me and my mess.
5. God abandoned me. He doesn't really care.
6. Who do you think you are accusing and challenging God?
7. God hates complainers.
8. Real love would give me a protection plan against pain. Anything this messy and painful can't really be love.
9. God doesn't really love you and true, pure love doesn't exist.

True, Pure Love

In Job, we catch only a glimpse of God's pride and joy in His son. In other Scriptures, we hear God open His heart with deeper feelings of a Father, Friend, and even Lover. God seems to keep His deepest feelings for Job suppressed from His adversary. Job, on the other hand, suppresses nothing; he lays the deepest beliefs and uncertainties of his heart raw and exposed before God. Yet in the midst of all this, we see the undercurrent of love for His Creator and Redeemer.

Job displays the typical response for his culture when he heard of the death of his children and the loss of all his wealth, until he "worshiped" ...

[20] Then Job stood up, tore his robe and shaved his head. He fell to the ground and worshiped, [21] saying: "Naked I came from my mother's womb, and naked I will leave this life. The LORD gives, and the LORD takes away. Praise the name of the LORD."

JOB 1:20-21, HCSB

5. What does this act of "worship" during utter grief tell about Job's relationship with God? How can Job's love for God be genuine if he spends weeks venting anger, hurt, and disappointment to God?

"Should we accept only good things from the hand of God and never anything bad?" So in all this, Job said nothing wrong.

JOB 2:10, NLT

[14] Why do I put myself at risk and take my life in my own hands? [15] Even if He kills me, I will hope in Him. I will still defend my ways before Him.

JOB 13:14-15, HCSB

[14] Can the dead live again? If so, this would give me hope through all my years of struggle, and I would eagerly await the release of death. [15] You [God] would call and I would answer, and you would yearn for me, your handiwork. [16] For then you would guard my steps, instead of watching for my sins.

JOB 14:14-16, NLT

[25] I know that my Redeemer lives, and that in the end he will stand upon the earth. [26] And after my skin has been destroyed, yet in my flesh I will see God; [27] I myself will see him with my own eyes—I, and not another. How my heart yearns within me! Even after my skin has been destroyed, yet I will see God in my flesh. [27] I will see Him myself; my eyes will look at Him, and not as a stranger. My heart longs within me.

JOB 19:25-27, HCSB

6. How does Job's view of God's love relate to his circumstances and suffering? According to 13:15 and 19:25-27, what drives Job's hope?

7. What does Satan stand to lose if Job's love is true? How does our true love for God and each other defeat the Villain?

8. Compare traditional wedding vows to Blake's poem and Job's response in suffering. Why is it good and healthy times can't show the strength of love like times of difficulty and sickness?

9. Why do you think we long for true love? What would happen in our hearts if we believe that true, pure love is a lie?

> "Love seeketh not itself to please,
>
> Nor for itself hath any care.
>
> But for another gives its ease,
>
> And builds a Heaven in Hell's despair."
>
> - *"The Clod and the Pebble"* by William Blake

If Job and others can love God in truth and God can love man in all his messiness, that would mean Satan's dream to fragment us, cause an eternal rift, and damage God's heart.

In *A Sacred Sorrow*, Michael Card writes, "Worship is not only about good feelings, joy, and prosperity, though they are at the heart of it. If this were true, then according to this modern American understanding of worship, the poor have nothing to say, nothing of value to bring to God.

We reason, 'Who could possibly conceive of a God who would want to receive such worthless empty offerings?' But Job desperately clings to such a God, one who encourages us to offer everything to Him, every joy and every sorrow. All our broken hearts. All our contrite spirits. Because he is *worth* it." [3]

 ## THE HEARTBEAT OF THE STORY

15-20 MINUTES

Unbearable Love

> "Love ... You can search the farthest reaches of the universe and never find anything more beautiful."
>
> - *Yvaine, the star in* Stardust

In *Stardust*, Tristan (Charlie Cox) chases a fallen star to win the heart of a beautiful, but demanding and immature woman. He finds the star transformed into a woman named Yvaine (Claire Danes).

As the two strive to overcome evil, Tristan's quest changes. He must distinguish between distorted love and true love, and then decide which he really wants.

Yvaine calls love "unconditional," but also "unpredictable, unexpected, uncontrollable, unbearable."

1. Why would Yvaine refer to love as something "beautiful" and also as "unbearable"?

Yvaine description of love is powerful: "My heart ... It feels like my chest can barely contain it. Like it's trying to escape because it doesn't belong to me any more. It belongs to you. And if you wanted it, I'd wish for nothing in exchange – no gifts. No goods. No demonstrations of devotion. Nothing but knowing you loved me too. Just your heart, in exchange for mine."

2. Again within smaller subgroups, take about five minutes to revisit your "true love" and "twisted love" charts. Now with more insights into love, add to or change items on your charts.

TRUE OR PURE LOVE	DISTORTED LOVE
1. Uncontrollable	1. Measured & careful
2. Focused on the other and his/her best	2. Focused on self and comfort
3.	3.
4.	4.
5.	5.
6.	6.
7.	7.
8.	8.
9.	9.
10.	10.

← **GROUP EXPERIENCE 1**

- SET UP DVD PLAYER TO SHOW A CLIP FROM *STARDUST* (2007)
- READ ALOUD THE "UNBEARABLE LOVE" INTRODUCTION
- PLAY THE MIDDLE OF SCENE 13 WHERE CLAIRE DANES IS TALKING TO THE MOUSE
- SHOW THE CLIP FROM 1:26:10 TO 1:30:28 ON THE DVD TIMER

"The greatest tragedy of life is not that men perish, but that they cease to love."

- *W. Somerset Maugham*

← **GROUP EXPERIENCE 2**

- DIVIDE INTO SUBGROUPS OF 3-4 PEOPLE EACH
- USE LARGE SHEETS OF PAPER OR POSTER BOARDS TO CAPTURE EACH SUBGROUP'S IDEAS

AFTER 5 MINUTES, GATHER TOGETHER AS A FULL GROUP TO DISCUSS EACH SUBGROUP'S NEW INSIGHTS.

3. Although Job suffers, doubts, fears, struggles,
   and contends with God, he still dared to trust
   God's heart and hope in Him. What do you think
   he held onto that kept him engaged?

4. Honest love that laments wounds and hurts is
   different from a business-like love that makes
   happiness and mutual benefit its center. What
   false beliefs or forces have encouraged you to
   keep your honest thoughts away from God?

Worship and Prayer Requests

**Spend a couple of minutes together in "worship,"
opening your hearts to God who is worthy of
your heart—lamenting, contending, or even
complaining about the messiness of your lives.
End by rejoicing that God does not abandon you
no matter how bad things get.**

Record specific group prayer requests and pray
regularly for them between now and the next
session. Consider ways to encourage one another
this week.

TAKE-HOME ACTIVITIES:

- "REFLECTION" IS
  EXPANDED SO THERE'S
  NO "EXPERIENCE"
  THIS WEEK

- REVIEW THE "EXTRA
  STUDY" SECTION ONLY
  IF YOU'VE SPENT AMPLE
  TIME ON "REFLECTION"

Notes:

2. John Eldredge, *Epic: The Story God is Telling* (Nashville:
   Thomas Nelson, 2007).

3. Michael Card, A Sacred Sorrow (Colorado Springs, CO: Nav-
   Press, 2005), p. 51.

CONNECTING WITH MY STORY THIS WEEK

 REFLECTION – QUESTIONS TO TAKE TO MY HEART

"If thou must love me, let it be for nought except for love's sake only. Do not say, 'I love her for her smile—her look—her way of speaking gently, for a trick of thought that falls in well with mine, and certes brought a sense of pleasant ease on such a day' for these things in themselves, beloved, may be changed, or change for thee, and love, so wrought may be unwrought so. Neither love me for thine own dear pity's wiping my cheeks dry, a creature might forget to weep, who bore thy comfort long, and lose thy love thereby! But love me for love's sake, that evermore thou mayest love on, through love's eternity."

- Elizabeth Barrett Browning, 1806-1861

- How "unbearable" is my love for God? Do I love God truly for Himself or do I love the blessings, positive feelings, and future rewards He offers?

- Has religious experience given me a false, ever-smiling, ever-blessing image of God? Do I love really love God more like Job or the three friends?

EXPERIENCE
GOD'S EXPRESSIONS OF LOVE

The villain was trying to poison the good things about Job and Job's love for God. He's doing the same thing to you. Meditate on these truths from God about His true love for you.

¹⁰ My love calls to me: [God as our Lover:] Arise, my darling. Come away, my beautiful one. ¹¹ For now the winter is past; the rain has ended and gone away. ¹² The blossoms appear in the countryside. The time of singing has come, and the turtledove's cooing is heard in our land. ¹³ The fig tree ripens its figs; the blossoming vines give off their fragrance. Arise, my darling. Come away, my beautiful one.

SONG OF SONGS 2:10-13, HCSB

The LORD your God is with you, he is mighty to save. He will take great delight in you, he will quiet you with his love, he will rejoice over you with singing.

ZEPHANIAH 3:17, NIV

⁸ Oh, how can I give you up, Israel? How can I let you go? ... My heart is torn within me, and my compassion overflows. ⁹ No, I will not unleash my fierce anger. ... for I am God and not a mere mortal. I am the Holy One living among you, and I will not come to destroy.

HOSEA 11:8-9, NLT

¹⁶ The Spirit Himself testifies together with our spirit that we are God's children, ¹⁷ and if children, also heirs—heirs of God and co-heirs with Christ —seeing that we suffer with Him so that we may also be glorified with Him.

ROMANS 8:16-17, HCSB

²⁹ For those He foreknew He also predestined to be conformed to the image of His Son, so that He would be the firstborn among many brothers. ³⁰ And those He predestined, He also called; and those He called, He also justified; and those He justified, He also glorified. ³¹ What then are we to say about these things? If God is for us, who is against us?

ROMANS 8:29-31, HCSB

After you allow yourself to bask in the pure love of God for you, take a few minutes to write a poem about love and God or a short love letter to the One who wants to exchange hearts with you.

EXTRA STUDY- RISKS, DOUBTS, DANGERS, AND HONEST LOVE

The Painful Realities of Life: Psalm 73:1-9

- What's the apparent contradiction between verse 1 and verses 3-4?

- What's the effect of painful reality on the psalmist in verse 2?

- On the one hand, we believe "crime doesn't pay," but on the other, there is the reality of verses 4-9.

- Why does the prosperity of the arrogant bother us?

The Way of Lament: Psalm 13

- Paraphrase the first verse:

- The psalms were used in ancient Israel during times of corporate worship. Can you think of any church songs like Psalm 13?

- How does verse 3 begin to change the direction of this psalm?

- How could the rejoicing in verses 5-6 come out of the laments in 1-4?

Job Laments: Job 3:1-26

- Paraphrase verses 3-4:

- From Job 1 and 2, list the many tragedies that befell Job:

- Have you known people who have experienced Job-like tragedy? Have you? List some examples:

- Compare Psalm 13:1 and Job 3:11. Does one seem more "allowable" as a prayer than the other? Why?

- Does Job 3 challenge your notions of mourning and suffering?

Job and the Arrows of the Enemy: Job 6:1-4

- How do Job's tragedies (verse 2) compare to others you have known?

- How is an arrow wound a good image of emotional pain?

- What is surprising about the arrows Job describes?

The Friends' Outlook: Job 15:1-16

- Why does Eliphaz make the accusation he speaks in verse 4?

- Is there any sense in which he could justify his statement in verse 11?

- What does verse 14 imply about the cause of Job's tragedy?

- How is the friends' perspective a neater religious explanation than the hidden reality of Job 1:8-12?

DANGEROUS ADVENTURES

AN EPIC

ROMANCE

VILLAINS & MONSTERS TO BE SLAIN

A BEAUTY TO BE RESCUED

BETRAYAL & INTRIGUE

BATTLES TO BE FOUGHT AND WON

UNEXPECTED TWISTS & TURNS

GOOD ULTIMATELY TRIUMPHS OVER EVIL

A HERO-REDEEMER

PARADISE

RESTORED

FAITH—REAL AND RAW

A MESSY FAITH

Therefore I will not keep silent; I will speak out in the anguish of my spirit, I will complain in the bitterness of my soul."

JOB 11:7, NIV

If I have sinned, what have I done to You, Watcher of mankind? Why have You made me Your target, so that I have become a burden to You?

JOB 7:20, HCSB

If only I knew how to find Him ... I would plead my case before Him.

JOB 23:3-4, HCSB

LARGER STORY SYNOPSIS

We carry an illusion that our lives are safe and supposed to be predictable. But we live stories of danger and intrigue. The Villain is at work. Pain and sorrow are real and raw! God yearns for us to open our hearts—the real and raw—to Him.

Grieving is a gift from God to help us cope and begin to heal from losses in our lives. Somewhere along the way we got the idea that God is without emotion so we should always relate to Him in a sterile, reverent fashion. Lament and complaint are some of the vehicles God provided to help us stay engaged with Him even when we carry deep pain and frustration. Faith is staying real and engaged until you hear from God.

OPENING SCENE

5-10 MINUTES

Which of the following action-adventure movie titles would your friends say best describes how you deal with life? Why do you agree or disagree with your friends' assessment?

❐ *Star Wars IV: A New Hope*—I'm optimistic despite the odds

❐ *Eragon*—The dragon scales are tearing me up

❐ *Raiders of the Lost Ark*—If I keep moving I stay safe

❐ *A Fistful of Dollars*—No problem; I can throw money a it

❐ *Gladiator*—I can defeat the enemy if I stand with others

❐ *The Matrix*—I'm not really sure I want to have a clue what's going on

❐ *Terminator*—I'm unstoppable and I'll be back

❐ *Ghost Rider*—You don't want me to get "hot under the collar"

❐ Other: _____

> "Perhaps this story is not nearly as 'safe' as we'd like to believe."
>
> - *John Eldredge*, Epic

WHAT'S YOUR STORY?

5-10 MINUTES

HOW YOUR ➡ INDIVIDUAL STORY FITS INTO THE LARGER STORY

1. As you focused on true and distorted love this week, what did you hear from God or your heart about God's love for you and your love for Him?

2. If you completed the "Extra Study," how did Job's outlook on his tragedy differ from that of his three friends? Which seems more religious? Which is more honest, more driven by passion?

BEHIND THE SCENES

10-15 MINUTES

THE WOUNDED ACTION HERO

It's a powerful action movie, a real man-flick. The good guy is an amazing shot with his 9mm handgun. He picks off bad guys left and right while running and diving for cover. He even gets off one of those amazing slow-motion shots, with two guns blazing while he's flat-out airborne. Wow!

There are so many bad guys, but we know our hero will prevail. The bad guys couldn't hit the broad side of a slow-moving elephant in spite of their superior, fully-automatic weapons.

Then it happens ... the good guy gets hit. Is his wound in the face or chest or somewhere vital? Heavens no, it's a shoulder wound. He winces in pain and is out of action for about five seconds. Then he sucks it up and starts shooting again.

You yell as you watch the movie, "That bullet would tear muscle and shatter bone. How can he go on?!" Amazingly, he presses on with a vengeance. In fact, he keeps using that wounded arm and shoulder. He fights on, as if he's only been bitten by a mosquito. You shake your head saying, "Only in the movies."

 CONSIDER THE LARGER STORY

 NOTE

ASK A MAN IN YOUR GROUP TO READ THIS SCENARIO ALOUD TO THE GROUP. BE SURE TO OVERDRAMATIZE IT.

They offer superficial treatments for my people's mortal wound. They give assurances of peace when there is no peace.

JEREMIAH 6:14, NLT

1. Hollywood doesn't have a monopoly on treating wounds lightly. God criticizes religious leaders for superficial treatment of deep wounds. What are some ways well-meaning religion treats emotional wounds like a B-movie script?

 OBSERVE

CONNECT WITH ➡️
YOUR HEART

2. Has there been a time in your life when you felt church phrases and Bible verses were given as topical treatment rather than addressing your real issues? Share the highlights with the group.

UNFOLDING THE LARGER STORY

30-35 MINUTES

Raw Feelings: Grieving Over Losses

We often think of Job's suffering as short-lived event, but it actually lasted for an extended period of time—months. Some of his losses were highlighted in previous sessions, but there are still more losses as the Adversary continues the assault.

> *³ So I have been made to inherit months of futility, and troubled nights have been assigned to me. ⁴ When I lie down I think: When will I get up? But the evening drags on endlessly, and I toss and turn until dawn. ⁵ My flesh is clothed with maggots and encrusted with dirt. My skin forms scabs and then oozes.*
>
> **JOB 7:3-5, HCSB**

INTERPRET ➡️

1. What is Job grieving in 7:3-5? After months of enduring suffering as Job did, how might you feel about your life and about God?

> *¹³ He has alienated my brothers from me; my acquaintances are completely estranged from me. ¹⁴ My kinsmen have gone away; my friends have forgotten me. ¹⁵ My guests and my maidservants count me a stranger; they look upon me as an alien. ¹⁶ I summon my servant, but he does not answer, though I beg him with my own mouth.*

17 My breath is offensive to my wife; I am loathsome to my own brothers. 18 Even the little boys scorn me; when I appear, they ridicule me. 19 All my intimate friends detest me; those I love have turned against me.

JOB 19:13-19, NIV

2 I long for the years gone by when God took care of me, 3 when he lit up the way before me and I walked safely through the darkness. 4 When I was in my prime, God's friendship was felt in my home. 5 The Almighty was still with me, and my children were around me. 6 My cows produced milk in abundance, and my groves poured out streams of olive oil.

JOB 29:2-6, NLT

2. What complaints and accusations is Job directing at God in Job 19? What is the desperate longing of his heart (Job 29)? What is the deepest need for Job in this time of crisis?

7 Those were the days when I went to the city gate and took my place among the honored leaders. 8 The young stepped aside when they saw me, and even the aged rose in respect at my coming. 9 The princes stood in silence and put their hands over their mouths. 10 The highest officials of the city stood quietly, holding their tongues in respect. 11 All who heard me praised me. All who saw me spoke well of me.

JOB 29:7-11, NLT

> **He has stripped me of my honor and removed the crown from my head.**
>
> *- Job 19:9, HCSB*

3. How can the loss of honor and respect described in Job 29 affect a man? What's the value in grieving those things we've lost in our own personal situations and also in a fallen world?

Raw Feelings: Why Have You Turned on Me?

² If only my anguish could be weighed and all my misery be placed on the scales! ³ It would surely outweigh the sand of the seas—no wonder my words have been impetuous. ⁴ The arrows of the Almighty are in me, my spirit drinks in their poison; God's terrors are marshaled against me.

JOB 6:2-4, NIV

"God, why do you hate me?"

- Jim Carrey in Bruce Almighty *(2003)*

INTERPRET ➡

4. Although his friends disapprove, Job believes he has reason to accuse God. Whom does he blame for the losses and tragedies in his life? Why does Job plead for fairness and justice?

Isn't it interesting that the New Testament (Ephesians 6:16) refers to demonic attacks as arrows?

5. Job describes his pain as arrows from God. How are emotional tragedies and traumas similar to arrow wounds? How are they different?

¹⁶ I despise my life; I would not live forever. Let me alone; my days have no meaning. ... ¹⁹ Will you never look away from me, or let me alone even for an instant? ²⁰ If I have sinned, what have I done to you, O watcher of men? Why have you made me your target? Have I become a burden to you? ²¹ Why do you not pardon my offenses and forgive my sins? For I will soon lie down in the dust; you will search for me, but I will be no more."

JOB 7:16-21, NIV

"Smite me, oh mighty Smiter."

- Jim Carrey in Bruce Almighty *(2003)*

Job isn't holding back with God; he's definitely "getting up in God's face." When Job lost it all, his wife encouraged him, "Curse God and die."

6. So what's the difference between what Job's wife was foolishly encouraging (2:9) and Job's messy and sometimes-disrespectful interactions with God?

Raw Feelings: Where Are You?

24 Why do you stay hidden and silent? Why treat me like I'm your enemy? 25 Why kick me around like an old tin can? ... 26 You compile a long list of mean things about me, even hold me accountable for the sins of my youth.

JOB 13:24-26, THE MESSAGE

When life is difficult, we are tempted to disengage from or dismiss God. This is often a form of self-protection.

20 I shout for help, God, and get nothing, no answer! I stand to face you in protest, and you give me a blank stare! 21 You've turned into my tormenter—you slap me around, knock me about. 22 You raised me up so I was riding high and then dropped me, and I crashed.

JOB 30:20-22, THE MESSAGE

7. Why do you think Job is so desperate to hear from God in his suffering? Recall a time in your life when God was silent and nowhere to be seen. How did you feel and how did you respond?

Raw Feelings: Going Too Far?

I will not restrain my mouth. I will speak in the anguish of my spirit; I will complain in the bitterness of my soul.

JOB 7:11, HCSB

"We must never lose sight of the fact that all of these laments [by Job] flow from the first faithful response in 1:20, 'Then he fell to the ground in worship.'" [3]

- Michael Card, A Sacred Sorrow

3 Yet I prefer to speak [directly] to the Almighty and argue my case before God.

JOB 13:3, HCSB

*³ If only I knew how to find Him, so that
I could go to His throne. ... ⁶ Would He
prosecute me forcefully? No, He will certainly
pay attention to me.*

JOB 23:3,6, HCSB

8. Job's friends condemn his lack of reverence,
   believing we must be very careful with God. How
   are Eliphaz' words the view of well-meaning
   religion? Why do people think expressing raw
   emotions to God is "going too far"?

Job is lamenting, grumbling, and challenging,
but he keeps talking to God. He stays engaged.

9. Why would gut-level communication be
   preferable to pious theology? Do you think God
   in His holiness can tolerate our raw emotions,
   accusations, and messes? Explain your thoughts.

Job's friends
have a lot to say
about God, but
only Job talks to
God. In times of
desperation, it's
God more than
anyone else we
need to hear.

The most damaging thing Job's friends do is to keep
him from lamenting—they distract him. "When he
stops lamenting, Job ceases to reach out to God. He
stops worshiping, no longer able to see that God is
worthy to hear his case. Lament is the deepest, most
costly demonstration of belief in God." ⁵

THE HEARTBEAT
OF THE STORY
10-15 MINUTES

Barely Hanging On

The movie *Signs* by M. Night Shymalan focuses
on tragedy and messy faith. After the death of his
beloved wife in a freak accident, Reverend Graham
Hess (Mel Gibson) discards his faith in God and

leaves the church. Six months later, he discovers gigantic crop circles in his field, which set the stage for an alien invasion of earth. With the help of brother Merrill (Joaquin Phoenix), Graham ends up securing his two children with him in the basement. His son is asthmatic and a scare puts the boy in danger without his medication.

1. Since his wife's death, Graham has not allowed prayer in his home. The depth of his pain and anger climax in the basement. How do you feel about someone speaking to God in the way that Graham does?

2. Graham Hess experienced a terrible and traumatic loss as Job did. How does his reaction to God compare to Job's in 10:13-18 (see also Job 7:16-21 earlier in this session)? Compare and contrast the way each man talks to God?

13 But you never told me about this part. I should have known that there was more to it— 14 That if I so much as missed a step, you'd notice and pounce, wouldn't let me get by with a thing. 15 If I'm truly guilty, I'm doomed. But if I'm innocent, it's no better—I'm still doomed. My belly is full of bitterness. I'm up to my ears in a swamp of affliction. 16 I try to make the best of it, try to brave it out, but you're too much for me, relentless, like a lion on the prowl. 17 You line up fresh witnesses against me. You compound your anger and pile on the grief and pain! 18 So why did you have me born? I wish no one had ever laid eyes on me!

JOB 10:13-18, THE MESSAGE

← **GROUP EXPERIENCE**

- SET UP DVD PLAYER TO SHOW A CLIP FROM SIGNS (2002)
- READ ALOUD THE "BARELY HANGING ON" INTRODUCTION
- PLAY THE END OF SCENE 18 "LOCKED IN THE BASEMENT"
- CLIP RUNS FROM 1:23:00 TO 1:25:55 MINUTES ON THE DVD TIMER
- IF YOU HAVE THE TIME, START AT 1:21:00 FOR MORE CONTEXT

"Don't do this to me again. Not again. I hate You. I hate You!"

- Graham Hess in Signs

God wants us to wrestle with doubts, fears, and accusations so He can plant truth and wisdom in our hearts.

"You desire truth in the innermost being, and in the hidden part You will make me know wisdom."

- Psalm 51:6, NASB

3. Do we need to be careful not to question or criticize God? How do you think God feels when we pour out our true, raw feelings on Him (see Job 42:7)?

The Bible warns against speaking to God with contempt and pride. Yet, even if we need to apologize to God as Job did, it's better to pour out our hearts to God than to shut God out or live a lie. If we refuse to live from our hearts, we will live in the fantasy of denial or the sterile prison of caution.

After the LORD had spoken these words to Job, the LORD said to Eliphaz the Temanite: "My anger burns against you and against your two friends, for you have not spoken of me what is right, as my servant Job has.

JOB 42:7, ESV

We don't have to be so careful with God the way Eliphaz and the others did, "walking on eggshells" as we try to protect Him and make sure that we get everything just right. Job risked acknowledging how he really felt. In the end, none of us "gets it right;" we're messy, life is messy, and the Villain is desperately working to pile up more messes.

Our relationship with God in not fragile! He cares deeply about each one of us. Working through the raw stuff of the heart *is* faith. Being careful and covering up is fearful and faithless.

Worship and Prayer Requests

Thank God together that He's not fragile and that your relationship is not reserved and prescriptive.

Record specific group prayer requests and pray regularly for them this week.

TAKE-HOME ACTIVITIES:

- THERE ARE 2 OPTIONS FOR THE "EXPERIENCE" THIS WEEK; ONE INVOLVES GROUP MEMBERS JOINING TOGETHER TO WATCH THE MOVIE SIGNS. PLAN THAT NOW.

- "REFLECTION" IS VERY IMPORTANT FOR YOU THIS WEEK

- REVIEW THE "EXTRA STUDY" SECTION ONLY IF YOU'VE SPENT AMPLE TIME ON "REFLECTION"

Notes:
4. Michael Card, *A Sacred Sorrow* (Colorado Springs, CO: NavPress, 2005), p. 50.

5. ibid, p.54

CONNECTING WITH MY STORY THIS WEEK

 EXPERIENCE – LAMENT

OPTION 1: Get Together and Watch the Movie *Signs*

Yes, *M. Night Shyamalan's Signs* is a story about an alien invasion, but the real story behind the story is the deep pain, messy faith, and redemptive struggle of a man with God. After watching the film together with other group members or on your own, discuss or journal your thoughts and feelings about the Graham Hess' journey through the mud. NOTE: *Signs* is one of four films you can delve into with Serendipity's *Finding Jesus in the Movies* small-group Bible study.

OPTION 2: Soak in Lament

Set aside a block of time to meditate on three psalms of lament: 6, 13, and 60. Then, write in a journal about the greatest disappointments in your life. Try to put in order the top three or four crushing blows you've experienced and describe them. How did they affect your life? How do they still affect you? How did you feel about God?

Review Genesis 50:20, Isaiah 61:1-3, Romans 8:28, and Jeremiah 29:11. Looking back, where was God and what good did He bring out of these deeply painful times?

 REFLECTION – QUESTIONS TO TAKE TO MY HEART AND GOD

How would embracing more of Job's messy faith change the way I relate to God? How willing am I to open up like that? What's preventing me from jumping into the mud with God?

God, am I really more like Job with a real and messy faith or am I more like Eliphaz and the others, treading carefully with You? How do You feel about the way I relate to You?

EXTRA STUDY- FORMULAS, THE UNEXPECTED, AND FAITH

Proverbs of Blessing: Proverbs 10:2-3,24-25; 19:16

What is true in your experience about Proverbs 10:2-3?

What is true in your experience about Proverbs 10:24-25?

What is true in your experience about Proverbs 19:16?

Many proverbs in the Bible and outside of the Bible are what we might call general truth. That is, they are generally true, but not in every situation. A great example is "crime doesn't pay." You might teach your children this while at the same time knowing some criminals have great wealth and do not get caught.

In light of this idea of general truth, how have you seen exceptions to the truths of Proverbs 10:2-3, 24-25, and 19:16?

Jesus Blows the Formulas: Matthew 26:36-46

Meaning of "sorrowful even to death" (verse 38):

Meaning of "let this cup pass from me" (verse 39):

Meaning of "betrayed into the hands of sinners" (verse 45):

Did the general truth of Proverbs 10:2 help Jesus? Explain.

How is the story of Jesus, the most righteous man ever, praying to be delivered from death an antidote to a simplistic view of blessing?

Ecclesiastes and Realism: Ecclesiastes 1:1-4, 16-18; 3:16-22

Meaning and thoughts in 1:1-4:

Meaning and thoughts in 1:16-18:

Meaning and thoughts in 3:16-22:

Ecclesiastes is a mature look at reality, rejecting formulas and seeking truth. Vanity or futility is the way life appears to be in and of itself. Wisdom disappoints because there are exceptions. Righteousness disappoints because we still die. Any meaning to life must come from above, not from within.

How does the perspective of Ecclesiastes help you avoid foolish expectations?

With Us In the Valley: Psalm 23:4

How is this verse ultimately more comforting than making a formula out of blessing?

DANGEROUS ADVENTURES

AN EPIC ROMANCE

VILLAINS & MONSTERS TO BE SLAIN

A BEAUTY TO BE RESCUED

BETRAYAL & INTRIGUE

BATTLES TO BE FOUGHT AND WON

UNEXPECTED TWISTS & TURNS

GOOD ULTIMATELY TRIUMPHS OVER EVIL

A HERO-REDEEMER

PARADISE RESTORED

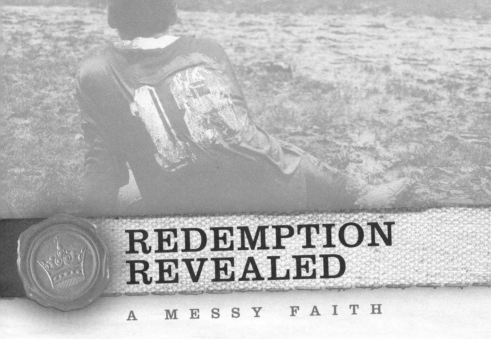

REDEMPTION REVEALED

A MESSY FAITH

Zophar: If only you would prepare your heart and lift up your hands to him in prayer! Get rid of your sins, and leave all iniquity behind you. Then your face will brighten with innocence. You will be strong and free of fear.

JOB 11:13-15, NLT (EMPHASIS ADDED)

Job: But He is unchangeable; who can oppose Him? He does what He desires. He will certainly accomplish what He has decreed for me, and He has many more things like these in mind.

JOB 23:13-14, HCSB

LARGER STORY SYNOPSIS

God's promises cannot be reduced to simplistic, predictable formulas. When God seems to act in ways inconsistent with His revealed character, we can experience disorientation and even despair unless we embrace a proper view of God and our present reality.

As we inevitably face suffering in our lives, the deepest questions of our hearts are not theological, but relational: "Where are You?" and "How could You? As we struggle to make sense of the messiness of life, we develop systems, repeatable processes, and formulas we can get our arms around. But we can't control or manipulate God, nor can we trust our circumstances as reliable indicators of our standing with God.

OPENING SCENE

10-15 MINUTES

1. We want a detailed map for life that helps us avoid unpleasant and dangerous obstacles on the road to our ultimate destination. Do you recall a time when you got lost in a strange place? Briefly share your story with the group.

"Surrender doesn't come naturally to me. I'd rather fight You for something I don't really want than to take what You give that I need. And I've beat my head against so many walls ..."

*- "Hold Me Jesus"
by Rich Mullens*

Quests, Grails, and Vexation

As legend goes, Arthur's kingdom was declining even as the king himself sank into depression. Sir Percival and the other knights of Arthur's round table set out to find the Holy Grail—the cup Jesus allegedly used at the Last Supper. They believed the Grail would heal Arthur and save the land.

Percival rode day after day in full armor, over every square acre of the land. He passed beyond weariness, into an oblivious daze. Yet he rode on and on, encountering potential answers, fending off grave dangers, and mostly fighting saddle soreness and hopelessness.

Yet the quest was doomed. Percival never found the Grail, although he came tantalizingly close once. Arthur died at the hands of his own son, and his body passed on over the mists to Avalon. The land was not saved and suffered more than before the reign of Arthur.

INTERPRET ➡

2. Although Percival had no guarantee of recovering the Grail, he willing set out on a perilous and grueling journey. Why do you suppose he pushed on even in discouragement and disillusionment?

3. Recall a time in your life that you when you were counting on a simple promise and it didn't come through. How did you feel?

← CONNECT WITH
YOUR HEART

4. How would judge Percival's success in achieving results? How would your response change if you evaluate success in terms of character?

← PERSONAL
APPLICATION

WHAT'S YOUR STORY?

5-10 MINUTES

← HOW YOUR
INDIVIDUAL STORY FITS INTO
THE LARGER STORY

1. What did you hear from God this week about the messy authenticity of your faith? What might God be doing in all of this?

2. As you studied blessing and reality this week, did you find anything discouraging? Were you encouraged in your look at reality? If so, how?

BEHIND THE SCENES

15-20 MINUTES

Maps and Formulas

In the fierce battle for people's hearts and minds, we must live as explorers in an untamed wilderness, blazing new trails through the danger zones created by the Villain. When explorers like Lewis and Clark put their canoes in the water, there were no signs, no maps, and no guarantees of safety. The explorers simply set out, minds focused on the journey and not so much a destination. Ahead of them lie beauty and danger, success and failure, joy and tragedy.

Preferring predictable adventure, many require a map—some guideline or formula that will help them avoid the traps and dangers life. Even when our formulas fail as they often do, many prefer them to a messy reality.

> *Zophar: [13] As for you, **if** you redirect your heart and lift up your hands to Him in prayer—[14] **if** there is iniquity in your hand, remove it, and don't allow injustice to dwell in your tents—[15] **then** you will hold your head high, free from fault. You will be firmly established and unafraid. [17] Your life will be brighter than noonday; its darkness will be like the morning.*
>
> **JOB 11:13-15,17, HCSB** (EMPHASIS ADDED)

> *Elihu: [10] He opens their ears to correction and insists they repent from iniquity. [11] **If** they serve Him obediently, [**then**] they will end their days in prosperity and their years in happiness. [12] But **if** they do not obey, [**then**] they will cross the river of death and die without knowledge.*
>
> **JOB 36:10-12, HCSB** (EMPHASIS ADDED)

For Job's friends, there is no story, no mystery, no messiness ... just futile attempts to control blessing and suffering. They are adamant about prevent suffering and increasing blessing.

1. How would you summarize the "blessing formula" in which Job's friends believed? Based on this formula, what are factors or causes should precede blessings in our lives?

OBSERVE
INTERPRET

Eliphaz: ⁴ *Is it because you're so pious that he accuses you and brings judgment against you?* ⁵ *No, it's because of your wickedness! There's no limit to your sins. ...* ¹⁰ *That is why you are surrounded by traps and tremble from sudden fears.* ¹¹ *That is why you cannot see in the darkness, and waves of water cover you.*

JOB 22:4-5,10-11, NLT

Bildad: ⁵ *The lamp of the wicked is snuffed out; the flame of his fire stops burning. ...* ¹⁹ *He has no offspring or descendants among his people, no survivor where once he lived.* ²⁰ *Men of the west are appalled at his fate; men of the east are seized with horror.* ²¹ *Surely such is the dwelling of an evil man; such is the place of one who knows not God.*

JOB 18:5,19-21, NIV

2. What do the words from Eliphaz (Job 22) and Bildad (Job 18) add to understanding the "suffering formula" that Job's friends espoused? Based on this formula, what are the causes that bring suffering into our lives?

INTERPRET

In my futile life I have seen everything: there is a righteous man who perishes in spite of his righteousness, and there is a wicked man who lives long in spite of his evil.

ECCLESIASTES 7:15, HCSB

PRINCIPLE OF RETRIBUTION

Theologians use this term to describe the notion that the righteous are blessed and the wicked punished. This principle contains general truth. Solomon writes:

"The LORD's curse is on the household of the wicked, but He blesses the home of the righteous."

- Proverbs 3:33, HCSB

3. How could Solomon write the words of Ecclesiastes 7:15, which seem in direct conflict with his words in Proverbs 3:33 (see margin)?

4. What are some examples you've seen of people who did the "right things" but did not get what they were seeking? Why do you think the "blessing formula" and "suffering formula" don't always work?

Too often, like Job's friends, we want to make God into some kind of mechanistic, theological computer program. God is infinitely more complex than we realize and the story has far more layers than we can even conceive.

God never intended His promises and principles to be reduced to simplistic, passionless formulas. We attempt to restrict or control the wildness of God and the unpredictability of this story. God's redemptive plan is complex beyond imagination.

UNFOLDING THE LARGER STORY
20-25 MINUTES

Disorientation and Disillusionment

A man promises his wife, "I will always love you." When he dies early in life, she can't help but feel betrayal … "What about your promise?" In her disorientation, she strives to gain control and, when that fails, she's bound to experience disillusionment.

22 Believe me, I'm blameless. I don't understand what's going on. I hate my life! Since either way it ends up the same, I can only conclude that God destroys the good right along with the bad. 23 When calamity hits and brings sudden death, he folds his arms, aloof from the despair of the innocent. 24 He lets the wicked take over running the world, he installs judges who can't tell right from wrong. If he's not responsible, who is?

JOB 9:22-24, THE MESSAGE

How frail is humanity! How short is life, how full of trouble! ... so you destroy people's hope.

- Job 14:1,19, The Message

1. Job refuses to give in to his friends' simplistic, heartless formulas. He knows he's blameless. What notes of despair do you hear in Job's laments? How can unexpected twists and turns in our lives cause disorientation and doubts about God?

⬅ **PERSONAL APPLICATION**

8 Your hands shaped me and formed me. Will You now turn around and destroy me? 9 Please remember that You formed me like clay. Will You now return me to dust? 10 Did You not pour me out like milk and curdle me like cheese? 11 You clothed me with skin and flesh, and wove me together with bones and tendons. 12 You gave me life and faithful love, and Your care has guarded my life.

JOB 10:8-12, HCSB

"Come to me in my dreams, and then by day I shall be well again! For then the night will more than pay the hopeless longing of the day."

- "The Longing" by Matthew Arnold

2. What inner turmoil do you hear in Job's complaints in 10:8-12? What doubts does he exhibit about God in 9:22-24 and 10:8-12?

⬅ **OBSERVE**

[7]Surely He has now exhausted me. You have devastated my entire family. [8]You have shriveled me up—it has become a witness; my frailty rises up against me and testifies to my face. [9]His anger tears at me, and He harasses me. He gnashes His teeth at me. My enemy pierces me with His eyes. ...[11]God hands me over to unjust men; He throws me into the hands of the wicked. [12]I was at ease, but He shattered me; He seized me by the scruff of the neck and smashed me to pieces. He set me up as His target.

JOB 16:7-12, HCSB

Sometimes God seems to act inconsistently with His revealed character. When this happens, like Job our hearts cry out, "I thought we had a deal God! What happened?"

3. Job's accusations mount as God continues to be silent through his ordeal. What aspect of God's character is confusing to Job? Do you think God sees Job's response as understandably human or as blasphemous? Explain your answer.

[3]If only I knew where to find God, I would go to his court. ... [8]I go east, but he is not there. I go west, but I cannot find him. [9]I do not see him in the north, for he is hidden. I look to the south, but he is concealed. ... [15]No wonder I am so terrified in his presence. When I think of it, terror grips me.

JOB 23:3,8-9,15, NLT

OBSERVE ➡

4. With the weeks or months that have passed prior to Job 23, what is Job's bottom line disillusionment with God?

The Cry of the Soul

[20]Only grant [these] two things to me, God, so that I will not have to hide from Your presence: [21]remove Your hand from me, and do not let Your terror frighten me.

[22] Then call, and I will answer, or I will speak, and You can respond to me. [23] How many iniquities and sins have I committed? Reveal to me my transgression and sin.

JOB 13:20-23, HCSB

Job struggles with the same two fundamental complaints we all face in times of disorientation and pain.

(1) "God, where are You?

(2) "God, if You really love me then why are You allowing this to happen?"

In the Garden of Eden, Satan tempted God's first beloved couple with lies about God's presence and the goodness of His heart (*hesed*). They chose to believe the lies and disengaged from God.

5. According to Job 23:3,8-15, how does Job's response stand in contrast to Adam's and Eve's in the garden (Genesis 3)?

Job stayed in the mess, fighting, struggling, complaining, and searching. God still dared to trust God's heart and God loved Him for it! God wants our hearts—honest, raw, and messy. He's annoyed by our facades of tidy, formulaic perfection. Job understood that God wants passion, not perfection ... honesty, not pretense.

6. Since God obviously didn't take pleasure as Satan did in Job's tragedies and ongoing suffering, why do you think God allows things to happen in our lives that He hates?

We can handle lots of things, but the thing that takes us out is God's absence or perceived abandonment.

HESED
A rich Hebrew word often translated "faithful love" or lovingkindness." It's used to describe God's core nature of unfailing, unending, passionate affection for others.

God allows things He hates, sometimes choosing not to intervene. God never promises to protect us 100% of the time.

7. Many people reject God at least in part because He doesn't protect us 100%. What do they need to realize about God's heart and the Larger Story?

Just as the blessings of Job's friends and the suffering of Job did not reflect God's love or their standing with God, neither do our good or bad circumstances provide a reliable indicator of our standing with God. Our circumstances may have nothing to do with us!

THE HEARTBEAT OF THE STORY

10-15 MINUTES

In his best-selling novel, *The Shack,* William Young chronicles the painful, but revealing journey of Mackenzie Allen Philips as he tries to make sense of his life after the tragic loss of his daughter. During a life-changing week with God at the site of his daughter's death, Mack spends time with the Holy Spirit clearing a plot of ground so the Spirit could plant something special in that spot.

Mack described the work like this:

"I mean, look at this mess ... but it really is beautiful, and full of you, Sarayu (the name used by the Spirit in this story). Even though it seems like lots of work still needs to be done, I feel strangely at home and comfortable here."

The Holy Spirit's response to Mack in the story gives us a lot to consider:

"And well you should, Mackenzie, because this garden is your soul. This mess is you! Together, you and I, we have been working with a purpose in your heart. And it is wild and beautiful and perfectly in process. To you it seems like a mess, but to me, I see a perfect pattern emerging and growing and alive." [6]

Because of so many influences, we're tempted to believe the lies that "God is not emotionally affected" and "God can't tolerate our raw emotions and messiness, much less enjoy us."

1. Mack has come a long way in seeing the messes in his life as something that might be full of the Spirit. How comfortable are you with the messes, struggles, and failures in your life?

← PERSONAL APPLICATION

"Though the questions still fog up my mind with promises I still seem to bear, even when answers slowly unwind, it's my heart I see You prepare."

- "I Still Believe,"
by Jeremy Camp

2. How does our natural focus on ourselves and our circumstances affect the way we judge whether something is good or bad? Why do you think God is so much more comfortable with the messiness of life than are we?

Job: ¹³ But He is unchangeable; who can oppose Him? He does what He desires. ¹⁴ He will certainly accomplish what He has decreed for me, and He has many more things like these in mind.

JOB 23:13-14, HCSB

3. In Job 23:13-14, how does Job explain how God and God's perspective differs from ours? What confidence can we find in this attitude regardless of our circumstances?

← CONNECT WITH GOD

In *The Shack* when Mack and Sarayu (the Holy Spirit) are spending time together in the garden, Mack has a revelation:

"I can see now that I spend most of my time and energy trying to acquire what I have determined to be good, whether it's financial security or health or retirement or whatever. And I spend a huge amount of energy and worry fearing what I've determined to be evil."

Mack is a modern-day Job. Job was the first righteous sufferer in Scripture—a forerunner and picture of Jesus.

Jesus Himself—
the sine qua non
of righteous
suffering told
us we would be
persecuted just
as He was (John
15:20) and that we
would find trouble
in this world as
He had (John
16:33).

"Lament keeps the
door open, keeps
Job on the dance
floor till the music
is over, until the
two tunes are
resolved ...
it is never about
winning the
fight ... only about
being faithful."

*- Michael Card, A Sacred
Sorrow, p. 45*

Sarayu responded, *"It allows you to play God in your independence. That's why part of you prefers not to see me. And you don't need me at all to create you list of good and evil. But you do need me if you have any desire to stop such an insane lust for independence. ... You must give up your right to decide what is good and evil on your own terms."*[7]

4. How can you relate to Mack's confession?

5. What do you think about Sarayu's perspective? Why is it so difficult for us to choose to live and rest only in the Spirit despite our circumstances?

Worship and Prayer Requests

Spend time together thanking God that He not only tolerates but enjoy our humanity. Thank Him for drawing us into a journey that is so much greater than simplistic formulas— it's a redemptive, relational journey in all its messiness.

Remember to hold one another up in prayer this week as you each seek to see God at work in the midst of your disorientation, confusion, doubts, and pain. Feel free to share specific prayer needs with the group.

Notes:
6. William P. Young, *The Shack* (Los Angeles: Windblown Media, 2007), p. 138.
7. Ibid, pp. 135-136.

CONNECTING WITH MY STORY THIS WEEK

EXPERIENCE
"I THOUGHT WE HAD A DEAL?"

Most of us are not aware of the deals that we've made almost subconsciously. We all have a set of beliefs that we intellectually assert. Buried deep in our hearts we hold onto deep-seated beliefs. These deals and beliefs surface when we face crisis moments.

Consider some recent struggles and disappointments with God—times when He seemed to act inconsistently with His revealed character. In a journal, list some important disappointments from your past as well as some recent ones. It would be insightful to write your own lament psalm about them. For style ideas, consider Psalms 13, 22, and 74.

REFLECTION
A QUESTION TO TAKE TO GOD

God, in what areas am I trying to play God in my own independence? What is it that I'm avoiding in my redemptive, relational journey that You want me to see?

EXTRA STUDY
COMMUNICATION GOD DESIRES

Piety vs. Lament: Job 5:8-9; 8:3; 11:7; 6:4; 10:2-3; 27:2

Job's friends say pious things about God in 5:8-9; 8:3; and 11:7. How would you paraphrase their statements? Do you agree with them?

Job questions God's heart in 6:4; 10:2-3; and 27:2. How would you paraphrase Job's statements? Do you agree with them?

God's Verdict on Job: Job 42:7

How is God's verdict on Job astounding?

Why are the three friends at fault in spite of their pious declarations about God? What does it seem God prefers to pious platitudes?

God as a Lamenter: Ezekiel 16:30-34; Isaiah 1:2-5, 10-11

In Ezekiel 16, God describes Israel as an orphan girl he found in a field. To what sort of person might you compare God from His words in Ezekiel 16:30-34?

Would you describe God's allegations against Israel in Isaiah 1:2-5 as calm prosecution? What is God's emotional stance?

In Isaiah 1:10-11, imagine God as the husband and Israel as a wife who brings well-prepared dishes to the table. God asked for the dishes (the sacrifices). So why is He disgusted with what His wife brings to Him?

Honest Lament: Psalm 74:1-11

What is reason for the psalmist's lament? How does verse 9 in particular focus the complaint of the lamenter?

Could you see yourself praying this way? Why or why not?

Trusting Lament: Psalm 13:1, 5-6.

How do verses 5-6 suggest a resolution to get through the doubt and confusion of verse 1?

DANGEROUS ADVENTURES

AN EPIC ROMANCE

VILLAINS & MONSTERS TO BE SLAIN

A BEAUTY TO BE RESCUED

BETRAYAL & INTRIGUE

BATTLES TO BE FOUGHT AND WON

UNEXPECTED TWISTS & TURNS

GOOD ULTIMATELY TRIUMPHS OVER EVIL

A HERO-REDEEMER

PARADISE RESTORED

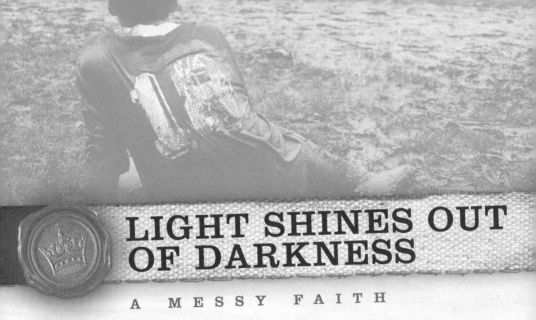

LIGHT SHINES OUT OF DARKNESS

A MESSY FAITH

Then the LORD answered Job out of the whirlwind and said: "Who is this that darkens counsel by words without knowledge? Dress for action like a man; I will question you, and you make it known to me."

JOB 38:1-3, ESV

Then Job answered the LORD and said ... "I have heard of You by the hearing of the ear; but now my eye sees You; Therefore I retract, and I repent in dust and ashes."

JOB 42:1,5-6, NASB

LARGER STORY SYNOPSIS

We don't have a bunch of rules and performance expectations. We have a living Redeemer! God longs for the day when we will trust His heart. He waits expectantly and works tirelessly for the time when we are ready to really see Him.

God may not require us to face the hardships that Job did. He relates to each of His children individually and uniquely. There will come a time when tears of pain and sadness will be no more, but in this season of the Larger Story the battle rages and the tears stain our shirts. Yet, even total darkness is light to God. In Him there is no darkness at all.

OPENING SCENE

10-15 MINUTES

We Love Happy Endings!

1. What's your favorite happy ending in any story or movie? What is it about this ending that grabs your heart?

REASONS A STORY DEEPLY MOVES US:

(1) It connects with the Larger Story God has written on our hearts.

(2) It connects with an element in our own personal stories.

2. How do you feel when a story does not close with a happy ending? Why do you think most of us are disappointed in a story that lacks a happy ending?

3. As Job's story comes to a close, it sounds a lot like a fairytale. In Job 42, what elements sound like "he lived happily ever after"?

"And he lived happily ever after to the end of his days."

- Desired ending for Bilbo Baggins' story in Fellowship of the Ring

4. Reflect back on Job's losses throughout the story. What things were *not* restored? With what losses did he have to grieve and cope to the end of his days?

WHAT'S YOUR STORY?

5-10 MINUTES

 SELECT EITHER QUESTION 1 OR QUESTION 2 FOR THE SAKE OF TIME.

1. As you connected with God and your heart this past week, what did you learn about lament? Would you be willing to read the lament psalm you wrote in your journal to the group?

2. What did you hear from God about your doubts and fears? About His redemptive, relational plan for you?

 CONNECT WITH GOD
WITH OTHERS

BEHIND THE SCENES

10-15 MINUTES

Our Cunning Redeemer

 CONSIDER THE LARGER STORY

Throughout Job's ordeal we hear him question God's presence, asking why his Lord and Redeemer remains hidden and silent. In the story of Ruth and Boaz, we find similar questioning and doubts.

The Book of Ruth chronicles the desperation and redemption of Naomi—and her daughter-in-law Ruth—after the tragic death of her husband and two sons. Despite Naomi's shattered dreams and deep struggles, she continued to watch for the activity of God in her life. When she saw God's hand at work, Naomi send Ruth to offer herself in marriage to a close family relative—a godly man named Boaz.

SESSION 7

HOW YOUR INDIVIDUAL STORY FITS INTO THE LARGER STORY

103

KINSMAN-REEDEEMER

In ancient times, land was people's lifeblood. Only men could own property. The single hope for a widow with no sons was a kinsman-redeemer (*goel* in Hebrew). A close relative could come to the rescue and buy back property lost or untenable and keep the family name/legacy alive.

SEE LEVITICUS 25:24-25
AND DEUTERONOMY 25:5-6.

PERSONAL ➡
APPLICATION

Despite Boaz' obvious attraction and admiration for Ruth, he responded with guarded caution.

> [12] *"While it's true that I am one of your family redeemers, there is another man who is more closely related to you than I am.* [13] *Stay here tonight, and in the morning I will talk to him. If he is willing to redeem you, very well. Let him marry you. But if he is not willing, then as surely as the LORD lives, I will redeem you myself!"*
>
> **RUTH 3:12-13, NLT**

1. According to verses 12-13, what puts the marriage offer at risk? What do you make of Boaz' contradictory statements and emotions?

The situation was not as simple as Ruth had hoped. Boaz sent Ruth back to Naomi. His response must have confused and troubled this young foreigner unfamiliar with Jewish law and customs.

> *Then Naomi said, "Wait, my daughter, until you find out what happens. For the man will not rest until the matter is settled today."*
>
> **RUTH 3:18, NIV**

2. What can we learn from Naomi's counsel when we feel like God, our Kinsman-Redeemer, is not responding or withdrawing from us?

Boaz went right to work, meeting with Ruth and Naomi's closer kinsman-redeemer in the presence of 10 city elders. In business fashion, Boaz presented the proposition of redeeming Naomi's property and, in order to increase his wealth, the man readily agreed. But Boaz didn't leave it at that.

⁵ Then Boaz added, "You realize, don't you, that when you buy the field from Naomi, you also get Ruth the Moabite, the widow of our dead relative, along with the redeemer responsibility to have children with her to carry on the family inheritance." ⁶ Then the relative said, "Oh, I can't do that—I'd jeopardize my own family's inheritance. You go ahead and buy it—you can have my rights—I can't do it."

RUTH 4:5-6, THE MESSAGE

3. How did Boaz show cunning in the way he closed the deal in Ruth 4?

OBSERVE

He was amazed to see that no one intervened to help the oppressed. So he himself stepped in to save them with his strong arm, and his justice sustained him. ... The Redeemer [goel] will come.

ISAIAH 59:16-20, NLT

Boaz serves as a forerunner of the ultimate Kinsman-Redeemer, Jesus. Isaiah 59 prophesies of Jesus a our *goel*.

4. What can we learn about God's heart for us from the story of Ruth and Boaz (Ruth 3 and 4)? What can we learn from Isaiah 59 about the way He works on our behalf against Satan, who would also lay claim to us?

PERSONAL APPLICATION

Through cunning our tireless Redeemer turns the tables on the enemy no matter what evil he sends our way. He did that for Ruth. He did that for Job. And He's doing that for you!

UNFOLDING THE LARGER STORY

30-35 MINUTES

Job Clings to the Living God

Job's love and pursuit of God is not pure, so in that sense it's not true love. However, Job's love for God is real; that alone makes it true and good and noble.

> ¹ **Job** continued speaking: ² "I vow by the living God, who has taken away my rights, by the Almighty who has embittered my soul—³As long as I live, while I have breath from God, ⁴ my lips will speak no evil, and my tongue will speak no lies. ⁵ I will never concede that you are right; I will defend my integrity until I die. ⁶ I will maintain my innocence without wavering.
>
> JOB 27:1-6, NLT

> **Job:** ²⁵ I know that my Redeemer lives, and that in the end he will stand upon the earth. ²⁶ And after my skin has been destroyed, yet in my flesh I will see God; ²⁷ I myself will see him with my own eyes—I, and not another. How my heart yearns within me! ²⁸ If you say, "How we will hound him, since the root of the trouble lies in him," ²⁹ you should fear the sword yourselves.
>
> JOB 19:25-29, NIV

Job refuses to settle for a simplistic or narcissistic view of God and God's plan for the world.

INTERPRET ➡

1. Job vows by "the living God" and triumphantly declares, "I know that my Redeemer lives." What might Job be thinking about God when he uses these phrases?

2. Do you get a sense that Job's trying to manipulate or appease God? How do you think he's doing at honoring God in Job 27:1-6 and 19:25-29?

← INTERPRET

Gods Invites Us into the Untamed

While Job wants answers from God, he refuses to try reducing God into a genie in a bottle that he can manipulate, control, or appease. Grasping that understanding in our innermost being is vital in deepening our relationship with God.

Job: ¹⁴ *Yes, I will take my life in my hands and say what I really think.* ¹⁵ *God might kill me, but I have no other hope. I am going to argue my case with him.* ¹⁶ *But this is what will save me—I am not godless. If I were, I could not stand before him.*

JOB 13:14-16, NLT

3. Job won't "curse God and die" (2:9), but he's willing to directly challenge God and die. What's the difference and what might drive this kind of thinking?

← PERSONAL APPLICATION

4. Verse 15 explains why Job would never curse God and die. Allow the thought to settle for a minute: *We have no other hope.* If God is truly God, where else can we turn? How might seizing that truth affect the way we approach God and life?

C.S. Lewis observed, "God whispers to us in our pleasures, speaks in ours conscience, and shouts in our pain: it is His megaphone to rouse a deaf world." [8]

It's often in times of suffering that God can draw us down unfamiliar and untamed paths that open unexpected journeys into deeper healing, more freedom, and closer relationship with Him.

³ He guides me in the paths of righteousness for His name's sake. ⁴ Even though I walk through the valley of the shadow of death, I fear no evil, for You are with me; Your rod and Your staff, they comfort me. ... ⁶ Surely goodness and lovingkindness will follow me all the days of my life, and I will dwell in the house of the LORD forever.

PSALM 23:3-6, NASB

I will lead the blind by ways they have not known, along unfamiliar paths I will guide them; I will turn the darkness into light before them and make the rough places smooth. These are the things I will do; I will not forsake them.

ISAIAH 42:16, NIV (GOD SPEAKING)

PERSONAL ➡ APPLICATION

5. What kind of relationship with God is required to follow Him down "unfamiliar paths" when you're blind or to walk fearlessly with Him "through the valley of the shadow of death"?

God Finally Speaks

Job has been desperate to hear from God. In God's own time, when Job and the others are ready to hear what He wants to share, God speaks.

"After all that I've been through, now I realize the truth that I must go through the valley to stand upon the mountain of God."

- "Mountain of God" by Mac Powell; performed by Third Day

¹ Then the LORD answered Job out of the whirlwind and said: ² "Who is this that darkens counsel by words without knowledge? ³ Dress for action like a man; I will question you, and you make it known to me." ... ¹⁶ Have you entered into the springs of the sea, or walked in the recesses of the deep? ¹⁷ Have the gates of death been revealed to you, or have you seen the gates of deep darkness? ¹⁸ Have you comprehended the expanse of the earth? Declare, if you know all this.

JOB 38:1-3,16-18 ESV

6. What was the look on God's face when He responded to Job in chapter 38? Do you think God is saying that Job has acted wrongly or been out of line?

> ⁶ Then the LORD answered Job out of the whirlwind and said: ⁷ "Dress for action like a man; I will question you, and you make it known to me. ⁸ Will you even put me in the wrong? Will you condemn me that you may be in the right? ⁹ Have you an arm like God, and can you thunder with a voice like his? ¹⁰ Adorn yourself with majesty and dignity; clothe yourself with glory and splendor."
>
> **JOB 40:6-10, ESV**

7. What tone of voice do you imagine God used when He spoke to Job in chapters 38–40? How does the message differ if you view God in each of the following roles?

   • Aloof Judge and Law Enforcer

   • Almighty Power who must put us in our place

   • Insecure Deity who bullies to demonstrate His dominance

   • Loving Parent who wants just wants us to trust the goodness of His heart

   • Lover who hurts when we doubt and falsely accuse Him

The typical view of God's words is that He's coming down hard on Job because Job needs to get with the program and start relating to God in the right way. This just isn't consistent with the story of Job or the God who reveals Himself as *hesed* throughout the Larger Story of Scripture.

It's easy because of our misunderstandings of God to think that God is blasting Job because he's crossed some legal line. But this story is not about reigning in sin or upholding some moral code; it's about our relationship with the living God who adores us!

It's About Relenting and Trusting

After correcting and reorienting Job's perspectives and beliefs about things he was sure he understood, God invited Job to respond. God was not at all satisfied with Job's first response.

> *3 Then Job answered the LORD and said,*
> *4 "Behold, I am insignificant; what can I reply to You? I lay my hand on my mouth. 5 "Once I have spoken, and I will not answer; even twice, and I will add nothing more."*
>
> **JOB 40:3-5, NASB**

8. Recognizing that God's goal is relationship, why do you think He found Job's response in 40:3-5 unsatisfying? How would you feel Job's shoes? In God's?

As God continued to expand Job's understanding, Job finally caught God's heart.

> *1 Then Job answered the LORD and said, 2 "I know that You can do all things, and that no purpose of Yours can be thwarted. 3 'Who is this that hides counsel without knowledge?' "Therefore I have declared that which I did not understand, things too wonderful for me, which I did not know." 4 'Hear, now, and I will speak; I will ask You, and You instruct me.' 5 "I have heard of You by the hearing of the ear; but now my eye sees You; 6 therefore I retract, and I repent in dust and ashes."*
>
> **JOB 42:1-6, NASB**

"It is true that relationships are a whole lot messier than rules, but rules will never give you answers to the deep questions of the heart and they will never love you."

- Sarayu to Mack in The Shack, *p. 198 .*

My heart is not proud, O LORD, my eyes are not haughty; I do not concern myself with great matters or things too wonderful for me. But I have stilled and quieted my soul; like a weaned child with its mother, like a weaned child is my soul within me. O Israel, put your hope in the LORD both now and forevermore.

- Psalm 131:1-3, NIV

9. In what ways does Job's response in 42:1-6 differ from his first response in 40:3-5? Why did God find satisfaction this time?

In order to lead Job still deeper into truth, freedom, and joy, God had to press Job until he recanted and relented—abandoning himself to the God. There is no safer or joyful place to be than with the One who loves you enough to never let go.

Because Job would not quit, he received many wonderful blessings from God throughout the rest of his life, but he never got everything back.

What Job received at the end of all his suffering was the most precious gift of all—He got God! In Job 19:26-27 Job yearned to "see God ... with my own eyes." Later in the story (42:5) when Job was ready, God lovingly granted his heart's desire: "now my eye sees You."

God is always focused on relationship.

Hagar, a servant woman to Sarah and Abraham also discovered the greatest treasure through intense suffering:

> Thereafter, Hagar used another name to refer to the LORD, who had spoken to her. She said, "You are the God who sees me." She also said, "Have I truly seen the One who sees me?
>
> GENESIS 16:13, NLT

Jacob found what he desperately needed after an extreme night-long wrestling match with God:

> Jacob then named the place Peniel, "For," he said, "I have seen God face to face, and I have been delivered."
>
> GENESIS 32:30, HCSB

Even though Job found blessing again, he never accepted the "blessing formula." He learned to accept the good and the bad as ways to draw closer to God and find still more in Him.

"In Job we discover a person who will simply not let go of God ... Job, like Jacob, faithfully holds on in the wrestling match of his life."

- Michael Card, A Sacred Sorrow, p. 39

111

THE HEARTBEAT OF THE STORY

5-10 MINUTES

One of the great mysteries of God continues to be that He brings life out of death and light out of darkness.

THE GROUP LEADER SHOULD READ THIS SCRIPTURE ALOUD TO THE GROUP.

⁶ For God, who said, "Let there be light in the darkness," has made this light shine in our hearts so we could know the glory of God that is seen in the face of Jesus Christ. ⁷ We now have this light shining in our hearts, but we ourselves are like fragile clay jars containing this great treasure. This makes it clear that our great power is from God, not from ourselves. ⁸ We are pressed on every side by troubles, but we are not crushed. We are perplexed, but not driven to despair. ⁹ We are hunted down, but never abandoned by God. We get knocked down, but we are not destroyed. ¹⁰ Through suffering, our bodies continue to share in the death of Jesus so that the life of Jesus may also be seen in our bodies. ¹¹ Yes, we live under constant danger of death because we serve Jesus, so that the life of Jesus will be evident in our dying bodies. ¹² So we live in the face of death, but this has resulted in eternal life for you.

2 CORINTHIANS 4:6-14, NLT

Relenting and Relating

OPTIONAL CLOSE 1:

OPTION 1: Dim the room lights. Stand or kneel together in circle. Spend some time inviting God to shine His light in Your hearts. Open yourselves to whatever unfamiliar, unexpected, difficult journey God needs to take you on so that you can "see Him with your own eyes" as Job did. Trade the simplistic formulas of religion for the messy reality of relationship. It's worth it!

OPTIONAL CLOSE 2:

OPTION 2: Complete the exercise individually.

Notes:
8. C.S. Lewis, The Problem of Pain, New York, HarperOne, 2001).

CONNECTING WITH MY STORY THIS WEEK

 ## REFLECTION – QUESTIONS TO TAKE TO MY HEART AND GOD

● What is still in the way that keeps me from trusting the heart of God enough to say with Job, "God might kill me, but I have no other hope."

● God, are You really willing to wrestle with me? What if I accuse You falsely or cross a line of respect?

● Are there areas that I've prayed about where You, like Boaz, are out of sight turning the tables on the enemy?

EXPERIENCE
CONTINUE THE JOURNEY

As a way to continue the messy redemptive journey you've begun with God through this group experience, choose one of the following books to read, absorb, discuss with others fellow travelers, and talk about with God. Be sure to keep a journal.

- *A Sacred Sorrow* by Michael Card (publisher NavPress)
- *The Shack* by William P. Young (publisher Windblown Media)
- *Shattered Dreams* by Larry Crabb (publisher Waterbrook Press)
- *Walking with God* or *Desire* by John Eldredge (publisher Thomas Nelson)
- Choose another study from the MORE series (publisher Serendipity by LifeWay)

The MORE series contains other great studies to challenge and help you on your spiritual journey. Consider another MORE experience that would most benefit your group.

REMEMBER

The most difficult part about any time of spiritual transformation is remembering and integrating insights and heart changes into your life. You can help yourself by setting aside times to prayerfully review your notes from this journey into Messy Faith. As you review your notes, continue to dialog with God and your heart. It's vital to keep a journal throughout this whole process of remembering. This will be a deeply rewarding time for you.

WELCOME TO COMMUNITY!

Meeting together to study God's Word and experience life together is an exciting adventure. A small group is ... *a group of people unwilling to settle for anything less than redemptive community.*

Core Values

Community: God is relational, so He created us to live in relationship with Him and each other. Authentic community involves sharing life together and connecting on many levels with others in our group.

Group Process: Developing authentic community takes time. It's a journey of sharing our stories with each other and learning together. Every healthy group goes through stages over a period of months or years. We begin with the birth of a new group, deepen our relationships in the growth and development stages, and ultimately multiply to form other new groups.

Interactive Bible Study: God gave the Bible as our instruction manual for life. We need to deepen our understanding of God's Word. People learn and remember more as they wrestle with truth and learn from others. Bible discovery and group interaction enhance growth.

Experiential Growth: Beyond solely reading, studying, and dissecting the Bible, being a disciple of Christ involves reunifying knowledge with experience. We do this by taking questions to God, opening a dialog with our hearts (instead of killing desire), and utilizing other ways to listen to God speak (other people, nature, art, movies, circumstances). Experiential growth is always grounded in the Bible as God's primary revelation and our ultimate truth-source.

Power of God: Processes and strategies will be ineffective unless we invite and embrace the presence and power of God. In order to experience community and growth, Jesus needs to be the centerpiece of our group experiences and the Holy Spirit must be at work.

Redemptive Community: Healing best occurs within the context of community and relationships. It's vital to see ourselves through the eyes of others, share our stories, and ultimately find freedom from the secrets and lies that enslave our souls.

Mission: God has invited us into a larger story with a great mission of setting captives free and healing the broken-hearted (Isaiah 61:1-2). However, we can only join in this mission to the degree that we've let Jesus bind up our wounds and set us free. Others will be attracted to an authentic redemptive community.

SHARING YOUR STORIES

The sessions of *Job: A Messy Faith* are designed to help you share a little of your personal lives with the other people in your group as you learn to parent well. Through your time together, each member of the group is encouraged to move from low risk, less personal sharing to higher risk communication. Real community will not develop apart from increasing intimacy of the group over time.

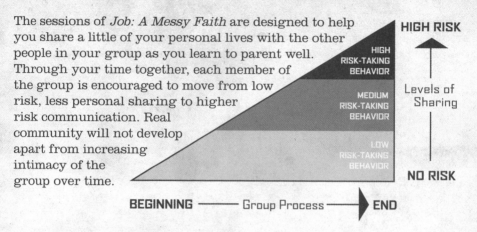

SHARING YOUR LIVES

As you share your lives together during this time, it's important to recognize that it's God who brought each person to this group, gifting the individuals to play a vital role in the group (1 Corinthians 12:1). Each of you was uniquely designed to contribute in your own unique way to building into the lives of the other people in your group. As you get to know one another better, consider the following four areas that will be unique for each person. These areas will help you get a "grip" on how you can better support others and how they can support you.

G – Spiritual Gifts: God has given you unique spiritual gifts (1 Corinthians 12; Romans 12:3-8; Ephesians 4:1-16).

R – Resources: You have resources that perhaps only you can share, including skill, abilities, possessions, money, and time (Acts 2:44-47; Ecclesiastes 4:9-12).

I – Individual Experiences: You have past experiences, both good and bad, that God can use to strengthen others (2 Corinthians 1:3-7; Romans 8:28).

P – Passions: There are things that excite and motivate you. God has given you those desires and passions to use for His purposes (Psalm 37:4,23; Proverbs 3:5-6,13-18).

To better understand how a group should function and develop in these four areas, consider taking your group a journey in community using the Serendipity study entitled *Great Beginnings*.

REQUIRED SUPPLIES AND PREPARATION FOR EACH SESSION

Session 1: Paradise in Turmoil

Supplies: Flip chart, poster, or whiteboard; markers; pens and paper

Determine in advance which questions you want to engage. In order to build a foundation for understanding the Larger Story, this session is a little longer than the others. This may necessitate abridging the group experience in order to maximize the emotional energy. If you do decide to take this course be sure to encourage members to take the time to interact with the content on their own.

Opening Scene: Capture the list on a visible flip chart or poster page to visually display responses. You'll also need markers.

What's Your Story: It's always a good idea to have pens and paper on hand for sub-groups or individual exercises. Provide five minutes for group members on their own to write descriptions of themselves in the style of Job 1:1-3 as if they're the main character in a story. How they'd summarize their place in the world, experiences, current relationship with God, and a few facts about themselves that make them unique will cover it well.

Pull the group together after 5 minutes. Take turns reading each self-description. As a group, note any interesting common patterns and distinctions. NOTE: Keep this moving and watch your time. If your group has more than 8 people, break into smaller groups.

Behind the Scenes: Capture the list on a visible flip chart or poster page to visually display responses. You'll also need markers.

Group Covenant and Group Directory: Take a few minutes as a group to go over the Group Covenant (page 123). Pass around your books to collect contact info in the Group Directory (page 128).

Connecting with My Story: Be sure to articulate the options given for the take-home experiences and extra study.

Session 2: The Epic Struggle

Supplies:
- DVD of *The Matrix* (1999)
- A DVD player connected to a TV

Opening Scene: Invite three volunteers to share the reading of Asaph's dramatic monologue; discuss questions as a group.

Behind the Scenes:
Part 1 ...
• Read aloud the "Through the Looking Glass" paragraph
• Prep the DVD player to show a clip from *The Matrix* (1999)
• Show Scenes 8, "Morpheus' Proposal," and 9, "Down the Rabbit Hole" (from 25:07 to 28:49 minutes on DVD timer)
• End after Morpheus pulls out a pillbox and says, "No one can be told what the Matrix is ..."
• Discuss questions 1-2.

Part 2 ...
• Ask a volunteer to read aloud the "Pulling Back the Curtain" paragraph
• Show a second clip from *The Matrix* (1999)
• Scene 12, "The Real World" begins at 38:39 minutes on the DVD timer
• End mid-scene (41:18 minutes on the timer)
• Discuss questions 3-5

Heartbeat of the Story: Encourage group members to spend a few minutes in quiet personal prayer. Remind people about the "Connecting with My Story" take-home experience and extra study.

Session 3: Dark Seasons and the Villain

Supplies:
    • DVD of *Spider-Man 2* (2004)
    • A DVD player connected to a TV

Behind the Scenes: Invite 2 to 4 people to take turns reading parts of Satan's resume aloud to the group.

Heartbeat of the Story:
• Set up DVD player to show a clip from Spider-Man 2 (2004)
• Read aloud the "I Finally Got to Him!" introduction
• Show Scene 30 "Jameson Gets the Suit" and the start of Scene 31 "Peter's Confession"
• Clip runs on the DVD timer from 1:08:09 to 1:10:00 (after Peter walks away from the assault)
• Discuss the group questions

Invite the group to engage in a battle prayer: Spend time together to identify and pray against the cunning assaults that are being launched into the lives of each member of your group.

Session 4: True Love and Distorted Love

Supplies:
- Flip chart, poster, or whiteboard; markers; pens and paper
- DVD of *Stardust* (2007)
- A DVD player connected to a TV

Opening Scene: Divide into subgroups of 3-4 people each. Use large sheets of paper or poster boards to capture each subgroup's ideas. Within smaller subgroups, take about five minutes to list various characteristics of "true love" and also characteristics of "distorted love."

After 5 minutes, quickly pull the group back together to discuss each subgroup's lists. Highlight those characteristics you see as central to true or pure love.

Heartbeat of the Story:
Group Experience 1 ...
- Set up DVD player to show a clip from Stardust (2007)
- Read aloud the "Unbearable Love" introduction
- Play the middle of Scene 13 where Claire Danes is talking to the mouse
- Show the clip from 1:26:10 to 1:30:28 on the DVD timer
- Discuss the group questions

Group Experience 2 ...
Again within smaller subgroups, take about five minutes to revisit your "true love" and "twisted love" charts. Now with more insights into love, add to or change items on your charts. Use large sheets of paper or poster boards to capture each subgroup's fresh ideas. After 5 minutes, gather together as a full group to discuss each subgroup's new insights.

Encourage group members to engage in the key elements of "Connecting with My Story."

Session 5: Faith—Real and Raw

Supplies:
- DVD of *Signs* (2002)
- A DVD player connected to a TV

Opening Scene: Ask a man in your group to read the "The Wounded Action Hero" scenario aloud to the group. Be sure he overdramatizes it.

Heartbeat of the Story:
- Set up DVD player to show a clip from *Signs* (2002)
- Read aloud the "Barely Hanging On" introduction
- Play the end of Scene 18 "Locked in the Basement"
- Clip runs from 1:23:00 to 1:25:55 minutes on the DVD timer
- If you have the time, start at 1:21:00 for more context
- Discuss the group questions

Encourage group members to engage in the key elements of "Connecting with My Story."

Session 6: Redemption Revealed

Opening Scene: Ask a man in your group to read the "Quests, Grails, and Vexation" mini-story aloud for the group. Discuss the related group questions.

Heartbeat of the Story: Read the short excerpt from the best-selling novel, *The Shack,* by William P. Young. Discuss the group questions and related quotes from the book.

Prayer: Spend time together thanking God that He not only tolerates but enjoy our humanity. Thank Him for drawing us into a journey that is so much greater than simplistic formulas—it's a redemptive, relational journey in all its messiness.

It's a good idea to remind group members to complete the key elements in "Connecting with My Story" this week.

Session 7: Light Shines Out of Darkness

The Group Leader should read 2 Corinthians 4:6-14, NLT aloud to the group. There are two optional closing exercises for this study. If your group is close option 1 may be best.

Heartbeat of the Story:
Option 1: Dim the room lights. Stand or kneel together in circle. Spend some time inviting God to shine His light in Your hearts. Open yourselves to whatever unfamiliar, unexpected, difficult journey God needs to take you on so that you can "see Him with your own eyes" as Job did. Trade the simplistic formulas of religion for the messy reality of relationship. It's worth it!

Option 2: Complete the exercise individually.

LEADING A SMALL GROUP

You will find a great deal of helpful information in this section that will be crucial for success as you lead your group.

Reviewing and utilizing these suggested principles and practices will greatly enhance the group experience. You need to accept the limitations of leadership. You cannot transform a life. You must lead your group to the Bible, the Holy Spirit, and the power of Christian community. By doing so your group will have all the tools necessary to draw closer to God and each other, and to experiencing heart transformation.

Make the following things available at each session:
- *Job: A Messy Faith* book for each group member
- Bible for each attendee
- Snacks and refreshments
- Pens or pencils for each attendee

The Setting and General Tips:

1. Prepare for each meeting by reviewing the material, praying for each group member, asking the Holy Spirit to join you, and making Jesus the centerpiece of every experience.

2. Create the right environment by making sure chairs are arranged so each person can see the eyes of every other attendee. Set the room temperature at 69 degrees. If meeting in a home, make sure pets are in a location where they cannot interrupt the meeting. Request that cell phones are turned off unless someone is expecting an emergency call. Have music playing as people arrive (volume low enough for people to converse) and, if possible, burn a sweet-smelling candle.

3. Try to have soft drinks and coffee available for early arrivals.

4. Ask someone with the spiritual gift of hospitality ready to make any new attendees feel welcome.

5. Be sure there is adequate lighting so that everyone can read without straining.

6. Connect with group members away from group time. The amount of participation you have during your group meetings is directly related to the amount of time you connect with your group members away from the meeting time.

7. There are four types of questions used: *Observation* (What is the passage telling us?), *Interpretation* (What does the passage mean?), *Self-revelation* (How am I doing in light of the truth unveiled?), and *Application* (What will I do to integrate this truth into my life?). You won't use all the questions, but be sure to use some from each.

8. Don't get impatient about the depth of relationship group members are experiencing. Building real Christian Community takes time.

9. Be sure pens or pencils are available for attendees at each meeting.

10. Never ask someone to pray aloud without first asking permission.

Leading Meetings:

1. Before the icebreakers, do not say, "Now we're going to do an "Opening Scene" question. The meeting should feel like a conversation from beginning to end, not a classroom experience.

2. Be certain every member responds to the "Opening Scene" questions. The goal is for every person to hear his or her own voice early in the meeting. People will then feel comfortable to converse later on. If members can't think of a response, let them know you'll come back to them after the others have spoken.

3. Remember, a great group leader talks less than 10% of the time. If you ask a question and no one answers, just wait. If you create an environment where you fill the gaps of silence, the group will quickly learn they needn't join you in the conversation.

4. Call people by name as you ask them to respond to questions or give opinions. Be sensitive, but engage everyone in the conversation.

5. Don't ask people to read aloud unless you have obtained permission prior to the meeting. Feel free to ask for volunteers to read.

6. Watch your time. If discussion time is extending past the time limits suggested, offer to the option of pressing on into other discussions or continuing the current session into your next meeting.
   REMEMBER: People and their needs are always more important than completing all the questions.

Group: Each group has it's own persona, made up of a unique set of personalities, backgrounds, and life experiences. This diversity creates a dynamic distinctive to that specific group. Embracing the unique character of your group and treat each person as a valuable member is vital to creating a living, breathing, life-changing group dynamic.

GROUP COVENANT

As you begin this study, it is important that your group covenant together, agreeing to live out important group values. Once these values are agreed upon, your group will be on its way to experiencing true Christian community. It's very important that your group discuss these values—preferably as you begin this study. The first session would be most appropriate.

Priority: While we are in this group, we will give the group meetings priority.

Participation: Everyone is encouraged to participate and no one dominates.

Respect: Everyone is given the right to his or her own opinions, and all questions are encouraged and respected.

Confidentiality: Anything that is said in our meetings is never repeated outside the meeting without permission.

Life Change: We will regularly assess our progress toward applying the "steps" to an amazing marriage. We will complete the "Taking it Home" activities to reinforce what we are learning and better integrate those lessons into our lives.

Care and Support: Permission is given to call upon each other at any time, especially in times of crisis. The group will provide care for every member.

Accountability: We agree to let the members of our group hold us accountable to commitments we make in whatever loving ways we decide upon. Unsolicited advice giving is not permitted.

Empty Chair: Our group will work together to fill the empty chair with an unchurched person or couple.

Mission: We agree as a group to reach out and invite others to join us and to work toward multiplication of our group to form new groups.

Ministry: We will encourage one another to volunteer to serve in a ministry and to support missions work by giving financially and/or personally serving.

I agree to all of the above_____ date: _____

ABOUT THE AUTHOR

MORE. Series Creator and Study Author – Ron Keck

Ron currently serves as publisher at Serendipity House as well as Managing Director of LifeWay Christian Resources. He is a graduate of Dallas Theological Seminary. He and his wife, Brenda, reside in Thompson Station, TN. Ron has written two studies in our God and the Arts series as well as *Song of Songs: The Epic Romance* and *Mark: Beyond the Red Letters*.

ACKNOWLEDGMENTS

We would be very much remised if we did now acknowledge the content of *Epic: The Story God Is Telling* by John Eldredge.

Contributing Writers: Ben Colter and Derek Leman

Art Director: Darin Clark

Cover and Interior Design: Scott Lee Designs

Editing and Production: Ben Colter, Scott Lee, Liz Gibson, and Melissa Finn

We are grateful to the editorial and design team as well as to John Eldredge. John's significant contributions to our understanding of the Larger Story has paved the way for experiences such as *A Messy Faith*. Authors Michael Card, Larry Crabb, and William P. Young have also been inspirations. It's our deepest hope for captives to be set free, broken hearts to be mended restored, the blind to receive sight, and the ashes of the story replaced by beauty (Isaiah 61:1-3).

GROUP MEETING PLANNER

The leader or facilitator of our group is _____

The apprentice facilitator for this group is _____

We will meet on the following dates and times:

	Date	Day	Time
Session 1	_____	_____	_____
Session 2	_____	_____	_____
Session 3	_____	_____	_____
Session 4	_____	_____	_____
Session 5	_____	_____	_____
Session 6	_____	_____	_____
Session 7	_____	_____	_____

	We will meet at:	Refreshments by:
Session 1	_____	_____
Session 2	_____	_____
Session 3	_____	_____
Session 4	_____	_____
Session 5	_____	_____
Session 6	_____	_____
Session 7	_____	_____

Childcare will be arranged by: _____

Other great small-group

SOUL CAFE
A guide to spiritual conversations.

Millions of spiritual sojourners don't yet connect with church or see it as the epicenter of their spiritual adventure. So if Christianity has become too scripted for you, pull up a chair at the Soul Cafe. This series, targeting people ages 25-45, helps you engage in your spiritual journey through biblically provocative conversations. It will take you deep into your story and help you discover the spiritual and often paradoxical truths of Christianity. Perfect for coffee shop, office, and lunch studies; or any informal get-together. Brave the elements. Share the quest.

Story. Narrator. Intrigue. 005117805
World. Justice. Utopia. 005126527
Unyielded. Undone. Unless. 005187236

FOUNDATIONS
Experience the mystery for the first time. Again.

Jesus seemed to love paradox and often taught by asking questions rather than dumping information. It's an idea we can all connect with—an idea we all struggle with. At some point in our lives, we've had questions—"Who is God" and "Where was He when...". God can handle these questions and desires the intimacy that comes from working through them. *The Foundations of the Faith* series takes groups through this process.

Foundational Truths
1574943111

Knowing Jesus
1574943103

The Christian in a Postmodern World
1574941089

God and the Journey to Truth
1574941097